MAGIC TIMES

Senior Authors
Carl B. Smith
Virginia A. Arnold

Linguistics Consultant
Ronald Wardhaugh

Macmillan Publishing Co., Inc.
New York

Collier Macmillan Publishers
London

This work is also published in individual volumes under the titles: *Believe It!* and *Feelings,* copyright © 1983 Macmillan Publishing Co., Inc. Parts of this work were published in earlier editions of SERIES r.

Macmillan Publishing Co., Inc.
866 Third Avenue, New York, New York 10022
Collier Macmillan Canada, Inc.

Printed in the United States of America
ISBN 0-02-131740-2
20 19 18 17 16 15 14 13 12 11

ACKNOWLEDGMENTS

The publisher gratefully acknowledges permission to reprint the following copyrighted material:

"Beach," from *Wide Awake and Other Poems* by Myra Cohn Livingston. Copyright © 1959 by Myra Cohn Livingston. Reprinted by permission of Harcourt Brace Jovanovich, Inc.

"Carmen," adapted from *Carmen* by Bill Binzen. Text and photographs copyright © 1969 by Bill Binzen. Reprinted by permission of Coward, McCann and Geoghegan, Inc. and Curtis Brown, Ltd.

"Clouds," adapted from *The Cloud Book* by Tomie de Paola. Copyright © 1975 by Tomie de Paola. Adaptation used by permission of Holiday House, Inc. Illustrations used by permission of the author and the Kerlan Collection of the University of Minnesota.

"The Dragon in the Clock Box," adapted from *The Dragon in the Clock Box* by M. Jean Craig. Copyright © 1962 by M. Jean Craig. Published by Grosset & Dunlap, Inc.

"Fields," from *In My Mother's House* by Ann Nolan Clark. Copyright 1941 © 1969 by Ann Nolan Clark. Reprinted by permission of The Viking Press.

"The Furry Ones," from *Feathered Ones and Furry* by Aileen Fisher. Copyright © 1971 by Aileen Fisher. By permission of Thomas Y. Crowell and the author.

"Henry's Pennies," adapted from *Henry's Pennies* by Louise Greep McNamara. Copyright © 1972 by Louise Greep McNamara. Used by permission of the publisher, Franklin Watts, Inc.

"I Have Feelings," adapted from *I Have Feelings* by Terry Berger. Copyright © 1971 by Behavioral Publications, Inc. Reprinted by permission of the publisher.

"I stand on the rock," (Cherokee Indian). Copyright © 1972 by Norman H. Russell. Used by permission of Norman H. Russell.

"Keep Running, Allen," from *Keep Running, Allen!* by Clyde Robert Bulla. Text Copyright © 1978 by Clyde Robert Bulla. By permission of Thomas Y. Crowell and Curtis Brown, Ltd.

"The Little Boy and the Birthdays," adapted from *The Little Boy and the Birthdays* by Helen E. Buckley. Copyright © 1965 by Lothrop, Lee & Shepard Co., Inc. Used by permission of G.P. Putnam's Sons.

"The Little Brown Bear," adapted from *The Little Brown Bear* by Cheryl Pelavin. Copyright © 1972 by Cheryl Pelavin. Used by permission of G. P. Putnam's Sons.

"Lucky and the Giant," adapted from *Lucky and the Giant* by Benjamin Elkin. Copyright © 1962 by Childrens Press, Chicago. Used with permission.

"Rachel," from the book *Rachel* by Elizabeth Fanshawe. Copyright © 1977 by Elizabeth Fanshawe. Published by Bradbury Press, Inc., and The Bodley Head. Used by permission.

"The Story Grandmother Told," adapted from *The Story Grandmother Told* by Martha Alexander. Copyright © 1969 by Martha Alexander. Reprinted by permission of The Dial Press.

"Taro and the Bamboo Shoot," adapted from *Taro and the Bamboo Shoot* by Masako Matsuno. Translated by Alice Low. Copyright © 1964 by Fukuinkan-Shoten. Adapted and reprinted by permission of Pantheon Books, a Division of Random House, Inc. Used also by permission of Fukuinkan-Shoten, Publishers.

"Undefeated," from *Street Poems* by Robert Froman. Copyright © 1971 by Robert Froman. By permission of Saturday Review Press, a Division of E.P. Dutton Co., Inc.

"Winifred," adapted from *Winifred* by Anita Abramovitz. Copyright © 1971 by Steck-Vaughn Company. Used by permission of the author.

Illustrations: Norman Adams, Tom Ballenger, Ron Becker, Heather Cooper, Ray Cruz, Tomie de Paola, Fuka Hervert, Robert Jackson, Bernie Karlin, David Klein, Ronald LeHew, Robert LoGrippo, Loretta Lustig, David McPhail, Pat Merrill, Sal Murdocca, Jan Palmer, Joanne Scribner, Stephen Tarantal, John Thompson, Philip Wende, Bill Woods, Ed Young. **Photographs:** Bill Binzen, Wayne Miller (Magnum Photos, Inc.), Victoria Beller Smith, Burk Uzzle (Magnum Photos, Inc.).

Contents

6

7

BELIEVE IT

There are many things you can do. You may be good at doing some things. You may not be good at doing other things. To find out what you can do, you must do new things all the time. It is very important for you to believe that you can do things.

In "Believe It!" you will read about a little bear who believes in himself. You will read about a girl who likes to make things. As you read, see if you can find other people who believe in what they can do. Can you do some of the things they can do?

The Story Grandmother Told

Martha Alexander

Part One
Tell Me a Story

Lisa said, "Please. Please, Grandma, tell me a story, please."

"All right, Lisa," said her grandmother. "What story would you like?"

"I'd like the one about Ivan and Lisa. It's the one about the green humming cat," said Lisa. "You know that one, Grandma. It goes like this."

One day Lisa and Ivan were on their way to a shop. They were on their way to get some ice cream. Then they saw a little man selling balloons. "Oh, let's get a balloon, Ivan," said Lisa. "We won't get ice cream this time."

"Mister, we want a balloon," said Lisa to the man. "Here is our money."

"Well, now, little girl," said the balloon man. "What balloon do you want? You can have one that hums. Just give me the money for the hummer."

Lisa and Ivan wanted a bright green balloon. They wanted a hummer, too. So they gave the man some more money for the hummer.

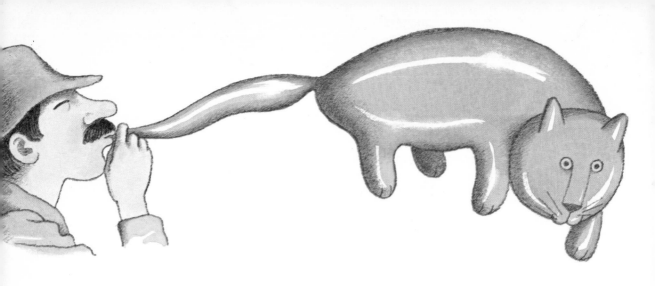

The little man put the hummer on the
balloon. He began to blow. He blew and
blew. He blew up a big green cat.
"Oh, mister, what a fine green cat!"
said Lisa.

The balloon man put a string on the cat.
He gave the string to Lisa. "Oh, thank
you, mister," said Lisa. "This is a fine
green cat!"

She took the string. The cat went up in
the air. It stayed behind Ivan and her.

Soon the green cat began to hum. Lisa
was very happy to have a humming green
cat balloon.

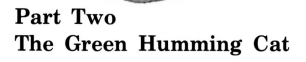

Part Two
The Green Humming Cat

Lisa and Ivan walked down the street.
They saw Lisa's friend, Annabelle. "What
a fine green humming cat you have," said
Annabelle.

"Oh, thanks," said Lisa proudly.

Then they saw Mrs. Goodman. She said,
"What a fine green humming cat you have."

"Oh, thank you, Mrs. Goodman,"
said Lisa proudly.

Joe and Mr. James liked it, too.
They thought it was the finest
green humming cat
they had ever seen.

HUMMMM HUMMMM HUMMMMM

13

Lisa ran home as fast as she could. She wanted to show her mother the fine green humming cat. Then —

BANG! The fine green humming cat was gone! Only little bits of green balloon lay all over the ground.

"Oh, Ivan, our new green humming cat friend broke! But that's all right, Ivan. You still have me."

"That's the story I want you to tell, Grandma. And here comes Ivan. He wants to hear it, too!"

"All right, Lisa," said her grandmother. "That's the story I'll tell."

And that's the story Grandmother told!

THE LITTLE BROWN BEAR

Cheryl Pelavin

Part One
A Not So Special Bear

At one time there was
a little brown bear who lived
in the woods with other bears.
The little brown bear thought
that he was very special. But one day
he saw that one little brown bear
looked just like another one.
It made him sad that he was
no more special than any
other bear.

From his cave, he watched a deer.
He saw the deer eating leaves off the
trees. He decided he wanted to be like
the deer. He would eat leaves off the
trees. That would be really special.

16

The little brown bear found
some branches. He went to his cave.
He put the branches on his head.
He made sure they couldn't fall off.
Then he worked at looking quiet
like a deer.

Then he went out to show his friends
what a special deer he was.
But the other bears just asked him
why he had branches on his head.

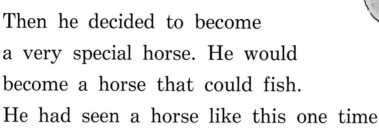

So he went back to his cave.
He took the branches off his head.
Then he decided to become
a very special horse. He would
become a horse that could fish.
He had seen a horse like this one time
at the lake.

This time he trotted a lot.
And he worked at looking like a horse.
He trotted out by the lake.
There he saw some horses and bears.
He was about to show them
how a horse could fish.
Then everyone laughed.
No one had ever seen
such a funny-looking,
silly little horse.

18

The little brown bear went back
to his cave. He decided
that being a horse wasn't
such a good idea. After all,
horses looked like each other, too.
Then the little brown bear
had another idea. He decided
to become a great bird
with wings. He wanted to fly
like a bird. That would be
really special.

He made some wings. He made
them out of branches and leaves.
Then he went off to a high place.
There he worked at flying.

At last he was ready. He wanted
to show his friends that he could fly.
It was a little scary, but he jumped.
All the bears on the ground looked up.
What kind of new giant bird was this?
Some bears got out of his way
so he would not fall on them.

The little brown bear did fall.
He landed on top of a big tree.
It had lots of birds in it.
All the brown bears laughed at him.
The little brown bear knew
he looked very silly. He thought
his friends would always laugh
at him. He thought his friends
would never want to see him again.

Part Two
A Special Bear After All

The next day, the other bears saw that
the little brown bear was gone.
They looked for him all day and all night.
But they could not find him. At last
they were so tired that they all
went to sleep.

When the bears got up, they had
a big surprise. They saw
a big, scary animal with big wings
and big ears. The animal had green leaves
all over it. And it had a long green tail.

"I am the Great Green Groasle,"
it yelled.

21

All the bears just looked
at this very funny animal. Then they
went off to talk about what to do.

When they came back, they were angry
at the Groasle. They thought
the Great Green Groasle ate
the little brown bear.

"He was a great friend to all of us,"
they said. "We loved him very much."

Then the Great Green Groasle
laughed. He began to take off
his Groasle things. He took off
his wings and his ears and
his long green tail. He took off
his green leaves. And there he was,
the little brown bear! He waited
for everyone to tell him how happy
they were to see him.

But everyone just yelled, "So it's you,
little brown bear!" And they all
went off. They were very angry with him.
Just his mother stayed. She told him
he was a very silly little brown bear.

But after two or three days no one
was angry with the little brown bear.
Now they knew he was really
very special. He had special ideas.
He loved to make up things.
He loved to pretend.

So the bears asked the little brown bear
to be the head of every bear party
and every bear play. It was his job
to make up things. It was his job
to pretend. The little brown bear
loved his new job. And all the bears
saw how good he was at it.

At last the little brown bear
knew how special he really was.

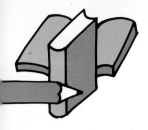

What Is on the Table?

A. Look at the table below. It shows the number of turtles and frogs that Rico found. It also shows where he found them.

ANIMALS RICO FOUND		
Place	**Turtles**	**Frogs**
By the road	5	6
In the lake	4	7

Read each question. Look at the table to find the answer. Then write the answer on your paper.

1. How many frogs did Rico find in the lake? __7__
2. How many frogs did Rico find by the road?
3. How many turtles were by the road?
4. How many turtles were in the lake?

B. Look at the table below. It shows the number of boys and girls that play after school. It also shows where they go to play.

PLAYING AFTER SCHOOL		
Place	**Boys**	**Girls**
At the playground	12	13
In the park	8	4

Read each question. Look at the table to find the answer. Then write the answer on your paper.

1. How many girls go to the playground after school?
2. How many boys go to the playground after school?
3. How many boys go to the park after school?
4. How many girls go to the park after school?

Lucky and the Giant

Benjamin Elkin

Part One
Giant Land

One morning Lucky went to the river
to catch some fish. But when he got
there, he had a big surprise. The river
was gone! There was no water— just dry
rocks. Lucky ran home to tell his father.

"We cannot live without our river. We
need water," said Lucky's father. Then he
went out to see the dry bed of the river.
"I will walk along this river bed
and see where it takes me," he said
to himself. "I will see if I can find
our river."

And he walked along until he
was way up in the hills. And then
he saw where the water from the river
was. The giant who lived in the hills
had it. He had put the river water
in back of a wall to make a lake.

"Well!" said the giant when he
saw Father.
"You have come for your river.
But you cannot have it."

29

"But I know the Law of Giant Land," said Father.

If I can do a giant's task,
The giant will give me what I ask.

"And do you know the other part of the Law?" asked the giant.

If the task you cannot do,
It is seven years of work for you!

"Do you still want to do the task?"

Father looked at the giant's shoes. They were not put on right. And they did not go together. "He does not look so smart," thought Father. "Not so smart at all!"

"I am sure I can do your task," said Father.

So the giant put one big foot
on the hill. And he put his other
big foot on Father's land.
"Let's see you do this," he said.

"That I cannot do," said Father.
"You know I am not a giant."

"Then you have to work
for me for seven years,"
said the giant. "Work!"
And Father began to work.

When Father didn't come home,
Mother said to Lucky,
"Where is your Father?
I will go and see if I can find him."
Mother went out to the dry bed
of the river. "I will walk
along this river bed and see where it
takes me," she said to herself.

And she walked along until she was up
in the hills. And there she saw Father
at work.

"Well!" said the giant when he saw
Mother. "You have come for your man,
but you cannot have him."

"But I know the Law of Giant Land,"
said Mother.

> *If I can do a giant's task,*
> *The giant will give me what I ask.*

"And do you know the other part
of the Law?" asked the giant.

> *If the task you cannot do,*
> *It is seven years of work for you!*

"Do you still want to do the task?"

Mother looked at the giant. His hat
was too little, and his coat was too big.
"He does not look so smart,"
thought Mother. "Not so smart at all!"

"I am sure I can do your task," she said.

So the giant took a rock and cracked it in two. "Let's see you put one rock into two boxes at one time."

"I cannot put one rock into two boxes at one time," said Mother. "You know I am not a giant."

"Then you have to work for me for seven years," said the giant. "Work!" And Mother began to work for the giant.

34

Part Two
Lucky's Pocket

When Mother and Father didn't come
home, Lucky said, "I thought Father
and Mother would be home by now.
I will go and see if I can find them."
Lucky went out to the dry bed
of the river. "I will walk
along this river bed and see where
it takes me," he thought.

As he walked, he saw many things
that he wanted. So he put them
into his pocket. At last Lucky came
to the place way up in the hills where
the giant lived. There he saw
his mother and father hard at work.

"Well!" said the giant when he saw Lucky. "You have come for your mother and father. But you cannot have them."

"But I know the Law of Giant Land," said Lucky.

If I can do a giant's task,
The giant will give me what I ask.

"And do you know the other part of the Law?" asked the giant.

If the task you cannot do,
It is seven years of work for you!

"Do you still want to do the task?"

Lucky looked at his father, hard at work on the giant's land. "Yes," he said. "I will see if I can do your task."

So the giant put one very big foot on the hill. And he put his other big foot on Father's land. Then he laughed and said, "Let's see you do this."

"Why," said Lucky, "that's not hard
to do. I have some of my father's land
with me." From his pocket, Lucky
took some earth that came
from his father's land. He put the earth
on the ground. Then he put one foot
on it. So now he had one foot
on the giant's land and the other foot
on his father's land. "Now, let
my father go," said Lucky.
"I have done your task."

So the giant let Father stop working.

Then Lucky saw his mother hard at work.
"I have come for my mother, too,"
he said.
"You have, have you?" yelled the giant.
"Then you have to do another task."
The giant took up a rock and cracked it
in two. "There," he said, "let's see
you put one rock into two boxes
at one time."

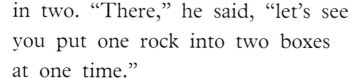

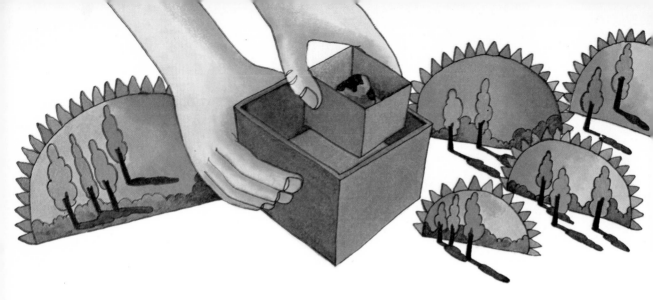

"Why," said Lucky, "that's not hard
to do. I have two boxes with me."
From his pocket, Lucky took
a very little rock and two boxes. One box
was smaller than the other. He put
the little rock into the smaller box. Then he
put the smaller box into the other box.
Now the rock was in two boxes
at one time. "Now, let my mother go,"
said Lucky. "I have done your task."

So the giant let Lucky's mother stop
working. There was one more thing Lucky
wanted from the giant. "We want
our river back, too," he said.

"Well then," said the giant.
"If you want your river back,
let's see you take all the water
out of my lake with a little spoon."

"Why," said Lucky, "that's not hard
to do. I have a little spoon with me."
From his pocket, Lucky took
a little spoon. And with it he began
to dig into the wall. Lucky dug and dug.
The water began to come out very slowly.
Then it came out very fast.
It didn't stop until all the river
was back in the river bed and the lake
was gone.

Lucky and his mother and father
looked at the giant. He looked so sad
that they were sorry for him. "Look,"
said Lucky to the giant. "There can be
water for everyone. Put a new wall
over here. Then you will have your lake.
And the water will still come down
to our land."

They all helped the giant make
a new wall. And by and by he had
a new lake. Then the giant
stopped looking sad. "You have been
so good to me," he said. "Let me know
if I can ever help you."

So Lucky and his mother and father
went home very happy. "Your father
and I are lucky," said Mother.
"We are lucky to have a boy as smart
and as good as you are!"

GIANT

One foot in the river,
   One foot in the lake—
What wonderful strides
   A giant can take!

The water goes "Squish"
   When he wiggles his toes.
Oh, giants have fun,
   As anyone knows.

His red rubber boots
   Reach up to his knee.
Why, puddles are nothing
   To giants like me!

—Elizabeth Sawyer

The Dragon
in the
Clock Box

Adapted from the story by M. Jean Craig

Part One
The Egg

One afternoon Joshua's mother went shopping.
She came back with a new clock. When she
took the clock out of its box, Joshua asked
her, "Can I have the box it came in?"

"Yes, Joshua, if you like. What are you
going to do with it?" asked his mother.

"Something," said Joshua.

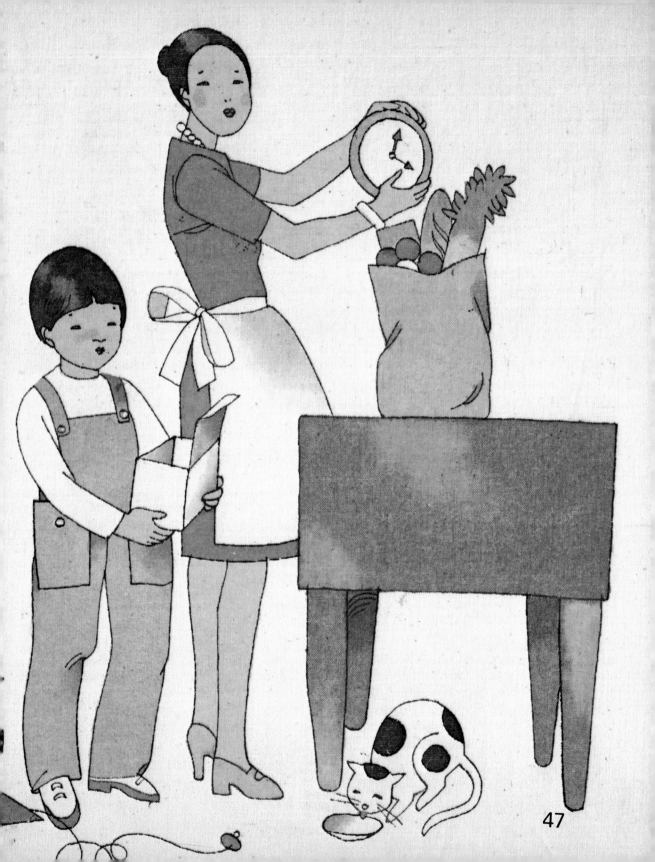

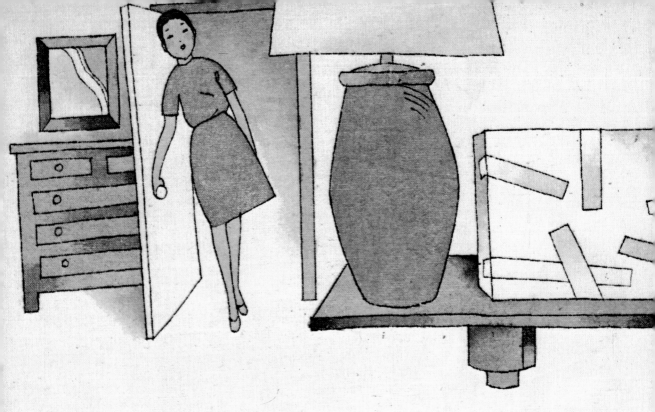

The next day Joshua's mother saw that he
had closed the clock box with a lot of tape.
She also saw that he had the closed box
with him all the time. He had it with him
when he was playing. He had it with him
when he was eating lunch. And that night
he put the closed box right next to his bed.

Joshua's mother came in to say good-night.

"Can you tell me what you have
in the clock box?" she asked.

"Yes, I can. It's a dragon's egg,"
said Joshua.

"Joshua—is it really?" asked his mother.

"Yes, it is, really," said Joshua, and he
went to sleep.

49

The next morning Joshua's father
asked him, "How is your dragon's egg doing
this morning, Joshua?"

"It isn't *doing*. It's just waiting," he said.

"What is it waiting for?" asked
Joshua's big sister.
"For it to be time," said Joshua.

"Time to hatch, you mean?"
asked Joshua's big sister, laughing.

"Yes, time to hatch," said Joshua,
without laughing at all.

"How did the egg get there in the clock box?"
asked his big sister.

"The mother dragon put it there," said Joshua.
"Before."

"Before? What do you mean, before?
Before what?" Joshua's sister asked.

"Before I closed the box with tape,"
said Joshua. And he took the clock box
out of the room.

Part Two
A Baby Dragon

Late that afternoon Joshua's father asked,
"How can air get into your box, Joshua?"

"The dragon doesn't need air yet,"
said Joshua. "It just needs to be quiet.
It needs to be quiet until it is hatched."

"When is it going to hatch?"
asked Joshua's sister.

"When it's ready to," Joshua told her.
"It will know when the time comes."

The next morning Joshua came down
to breakfast a little late. He put the clock box
next to his milk. There was a small hole
cut on one side of it.

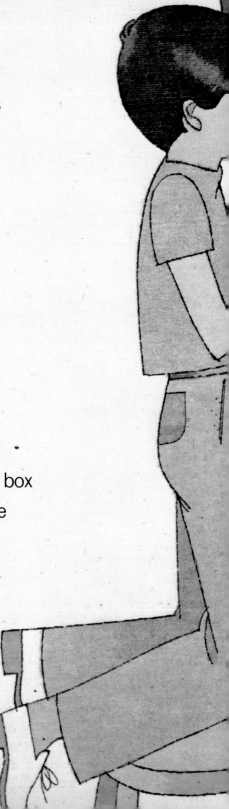

"He's a boy dragon," Joshua told everyone
as he sat down. "The egg hatched last night,
very, very late."

Joshua's mother asked slowly, "How could you
tell that the egg hatched? Did you hear it?"

"*He*, not *it*," said Joshua. "No, I didn't hear
him. He was very quiet. It was late
at night. It was time, and he was ready.
So I made a hole in the box just now.
He needs air."

"And now you can peek into the hole to see
what he's like," Joshua's sister said.

"I know what he's like," said Joshua. "He's like a baby dragon. A baby dragon just hatched."

"But you could look, just to be sure, couldn't you?" asked his sister.

"I am sure," Joshua said. "And he isn't ready for me to look yet. He wants to be all alone because he is still very little."

The next day, Joshua's mother and father and his big sister all had a lot of things to do. No one said anything about the clock box until it was time for bed. Joshua's sister and mother came in to say good-night. His sister asked, "Do you still have a baby dragon in that box, Joshua?"

"Yes," said Joshua.

"Have you seen him yet?" his sister asked.

"Yes," said Joshua. "Now I have."

"Say, that's great! What does he look like?"
asked his sister again.

"He's green, and his wings are very soft.
They have tiny gold dots on them," Joshua
told her.

"How do you know that his wings are soft?"
his mother asked.

"It's always that way with baby dragons,"
said Joshua. "They always have soft wings
with tiny gold dots on them."

Part Three
Where Dragons Go

The next morning,
Joshua told his big sister, "The dragon's
name is Emmeline."

"Emmeline! But Joshua, that's a name for
a girl!" said his sister.

"I know, but he's a Chinese dragon. And
Chinese boy dragons like to have girls'
names. His eyes are red. And his wings
are getting strong," Joshua told her.

"Can I see him?" asked his sister.

"No," said Joshua. "He is still too little."

"But you look at him now, don't you?" asked his sister.

"He knows me now," said Joshua.

That night Joshua's father asked, "What are you going to feed the dragon, Joshua?"

"They don't eat when they are little," said Joshua. "Not baby dragons."

"Well, then, what are you going to feed him when he gets big?" his father asked again.

"I don't think I'll have to feed him then," Joshua said.

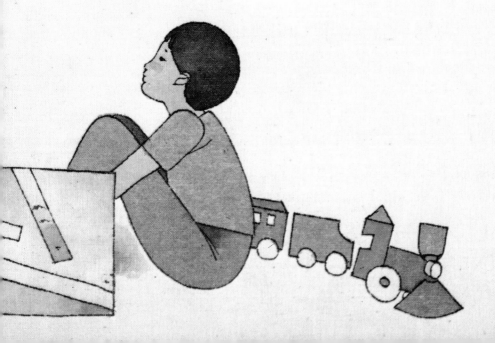

It was seven days after the day
Joshua's mother had come home
with the clock box. When Joshua came
down to breakfast that day, everyone said
"Good morning." But no one saw that
he didn't have the clock box with him.

That afternoon, Joshua's mother went up
to his room. She saw the clock box
by the window. The tape was cut off.
The box was wide open. She did not see
anything in the box.

"Joshua! Your box is open. Your dragon
is gone!" Joshua's mother called.

"I know," said Joshua. "He was ready
last night. And his wings were very strong.
He flew away."

"Did he really? But Joshua, where could he
fly to?" asked his mother.

"He flew to the place where dragons go,"
Joshua said.

Then Joshua walked over to the open box.
"I think this will be a very good box
for my crayons," he said. "I think I will
put my crayons in it right now."

And Joshua did.

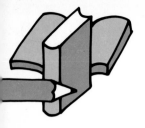

Mindy Gets a Surprise

Read the story about Mindy.

Mindy lived in a big city. She wanted a bike very much. But she didn't have the money to get one. Mr. Lucky's Bike Shop was on the street where Mindy lived. Every day Mindy went to Mr. Lucky's shop. She helped him with the bikes each time she came. Mr. Lucky and Mindy became good friends. One morning Mr. Lucky gave Mindy a present. It was a red bike with her name on it!

Read each question. Write the sentence that answers the question on your paper.

1. Where did Mindy live?
Mindy lived in a big city.
Mindy lived in the woods.
1. Mindy lived in a big city.

2. What did Mindy want very much?

Mindy wanted a dog very much.

Mindy wanted a bike very much.

3. Why couldn't Mindy buy a bike?

Mindy didn't see a bike she liked.

Mindy didn't have the money to get a bike.

4. Why did Mindy go to Mr. Lucky's Bike Shop every day?

Mindy went to buy a new bike.

Mindy went to help Mr. Lucky with the bikes.

5. Did Mindy get a new bike?

No, Mindy did not get a bike.

Yes, Mindy got a bike.

Winifred

Part One
Signs

Winifred made things. She made things
to play with and things to look at.
She made all kinds of things.
She made big things and little things.
She made anything at all.

Winifred made so many things. But she
made them all so fast that they
came out looking funny. And sometimes
they didn't stay together long.

Winifred gave away all the things she
made. She gave them away
to the people on her street.
But no one knew what to do
with the things Winifred made.

Everyone said, "Thank you," but Winifred
was not happy. She knew that people
didn't really mean "Thank you."
They didn't know what to do
with Winifred's presents.

One day the woman next door said,
"Winifred, I know you like to make things.
Why don't you make signs?"

"Signs?" said Winifred.
"What a good idea!"

Winifred always went right to work
on a new idea. The next day she went
to the country with her family.
She saw all kinds of signs there.

When she got home, Winifred sat
right down and began to work.
She made signs just like the ones she
had seen in the country. But no one
could use the signs. No one
wanted them at all. So Winifred put
the signs up on the outside
of her house.

The next day, all kinds of people
stopped in to buy eggs or flowers.
They asked if they could buy dogs.
They asked if they could buy the house.
People came to the house all day long
because of the signs. They got mad
and yelled at Winifred because
things were not really for sale.
So Winifred took down all the signs.
She put them in the garbage can.

Winifred was not happy. But when
Winifred began to do something, she
couldn't stop. Every time she saw
a sign, she wanted to make one
just like it.

66

Part Two
More Signs

One day Winifred went to the zoo.
When she got home, she sat right down
to work. She made signs
just like the ones at the zoo.

But no one wanted the zoo signs.
So Winifred put the signs
up and down the street.
The street was something to see.
There were red and yellow signs
everywhere.

The next morning Winifred looked out
of her window. She had
a big surprise. Many people were
outside in the street. Police officers were
there, too. People were yelling
at each other. They had seen
the signs. They thought that the animals
had run away from the zoo.

Some people looked scared. Some people
looked mad. Then Winifred saw
the woman next door. She looked
more scared than anyone.
The police officers began to take down
Winifred's signs. They put them
in the police cars.

Winifred wanted to run. Winifred
wanted to hide. Winifred wanted
to fly away. But she didn't.
She called from her window, "Wait!
Wait! Wait!"

Winifred ran down to the street.
"I'm sorry. I'm really sorry, everyone!"
she called out. "I didn't mean
to scare anyone."

BIRD
HOUSE

DANGER!
DO NOT
FEED THE
ELEPHANT

LION
FEEDING
5:30 P.

All the people in the street
stopped yelling at each other.
They all looked at Winifred.
Everyone was quiet.

Then the woman next door said,
"Things are going to be all right,
Winifred. You were a good girl
to tell everyone you made the signs.
Will you help me into my house?"

So Winifred helped the woman back
into her house. They sat and talked.
The other people walked slowly away.
The police officers drove away. They took
the last of Winifred's signs with them.

When Winifred went back to her house,
she had a new idea. She got out
her crayons and her paints.
She made a very, very big sign.

A friend helped Winifred put up
the sign over her doorway.

From then on, Winifred had a lot of work to do. She got an order from Bob Cook for his tree house.

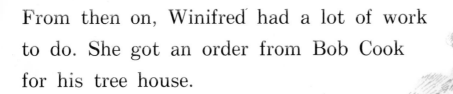

Then she had to make a sign for the people next door.

Next she made a sign for the new baby down the street.

You never saw such great signs.

One day Winifred made a tiny sign
for the woman next door. She wanted it
for her cat. The sign had the cat's name
on it.

At last Winifred was happy. Now people
could use the things that she made.
When Winifred made a sign to order,
people said "Thank you, thank you."
And Winifred knew that they
really did mean it.

Clouds

Tomie de Paola

The next time you go outside,
look up at the sky.
You may see clouds.

Clouds are little drops of water or ice.
They are in the air high above the earth.
If you could jump on a bird and fly way up,
you would see clouds all over the earth.

74

There are many kinds of clouds.
Some are high up. Some are in the middle.
Some are low down in the sky.

The three main kinds of clouds are called
cirrus, cumulus, and *stratus* clouds.
You can tell them apart
by the way they look.
You can tell by where they are
in the sky, too.

Cirrus clouds are white and feathery.
They are the highest clouds.
They are sometimes called "mares' tails."

Cumulus clouds are puffy.

They look like cauliflowers.

They are flat at the bottom, too.

Cumulus clouds are always moving.

They are low down in the sky.

 This is a cloud. This is a cauliflower.

Stratus clouds are low, too.
They are wide and flat and gray.
They are sometimes called "high fogs."
Rain or snow may fall from stratus clouds.

Fog is a cloud made of water drops.
It is a cloud on the ground.
If you live on a high mountain,
you may see a lot of fog.
Fog can come right into your yard.

Long ago, people looked at the clouds
and saw things.
People saw giants, animals, ships,
and castles, too!

There are some sayings about clouds.
They help tell if it will rain or not.
Here are some sayings for travelers.

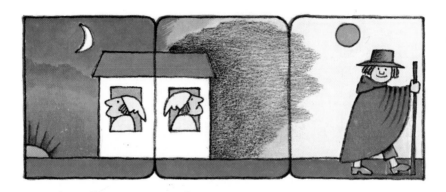

Evening red and morning gray,
Set the travelers on their way.

Evening gray and morning red,
Rain will fall upon your head.

So you see, there is much to know about clouds.

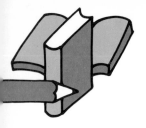

What Do You Hear?

A. Say these words.

found   last

Look at the two letters at the end.
These letters spell the end sounds.
Now look at the words below. Choose
the letters that will make a word.
Write the word on your paper.

1. playgrou___ ___   nd   st
   1. playground
2. fa___ ___   nd   st
3. frie___ ___   nd   st
4. ju___ ___   nd   st
5. behi___ ___   nd   st
6. arou___ ___   nd   st
7. mu___ ___   nd   st
8. ha___ ___   nd   st
9. mo___ ___   nd   st
10. ki___ ___   nd   st

B. Say these words.

<u>fl</u>ew	<u>br</u>anches
<u>sw</u>im	<u>sc</u>ales
<u>st</u>ay	<u>cl</u>own

Look at the two letters at the front.
These letters spell the first sounds.
Now look at the words below. Choose
the letters that will make a word.
Write the word on your paper.

1. __ __owers   br   fl   st
2. __ __ock   sw   cl   br
3. __ __op   br   st   sc
4. __ __other   st   fl   br
5. __ __ory   cl   br   st
6. __ __eakfast   fl   sw   br
7. __ __im   cl   fl   sw
8. __ __are   br   sc   cl
9. __ __oud   cl   st   br
10. __ __ayed   st   cl   fl

Rachel

Elizabeth Fanshawe

Today I made a birthday card
for my mother.
My teacher helped me.
I am in a wheelchair.
I go to school with my sister.

We have to work hard, but it's fun.
It was my turn to feed the mice
this morning.

When it's time to go home, we all
help to clean up.

Sometimes my friends like to push me.
But I can do it alone, too. I go fast
down the ramp.

My mother gets us at school, because I
can't get on the bus.
My chair goes in the car.

Some days, Grandma comes to see me.
She always brings something for my dog.

We all help to get something to eat.
My father sits next to me at the table.

On Thursdays, we go to Brownies.
I like the games best.

I can almost swim without help now.
Someday soon, I am going to learn to
ride a horse, too.

Last year we went to the mountains.
Everyone laughed when they saw
the pictures I took.

90

My father and I talk about
what I will be when I grow up.
There are so many things I could be.

Where's the Dog?

Bernice Myers

Part One
The Cat

Willie found a cat
on the road
and took him home.

"No cats," said his father.

"Your father is right,"
said his mother.

"Please, can't he stay?"
asked Willie.
"Suzy and I
will take care of him.
Please, please? Yes?
We **can** keep him? Great!"

Suzy ran to the cat
with some milk.
When the milk was gone,
Suzy took the cat on her lap.

"Nice cat," she said.

"Now, let me hold the cat,"
said Willie.

"No!
It's still my turn,"
said Suzy.

"Let me have a turn
right now," said Willie.
"I'm the one who found
the cat!"
Willie took the cat
away from Suzy.

"Can I hold him now?"
asked Suzy.
"Are you going to give
him to me?"

"No! He is mine!"
yelled Willie.
"I found him.
Go get another pet
if you want one
so much."

Suzy ran to her room.
"I will!" she thought.
"I'll get a pet
that will be just mine."

Part Two
Howard

Suzy walked down
the road.
After a long time
she still had not found
a pet.
She sat down to think.

Soon, she was pulling
a rope with a loop
at the end of it.

When she got home,
she said to her mother,
"Watch out for Howard."

Suzy's mother
didn't see anything
but a rope with a loop
at the end of it.
"Howard? Who's Howard?"
she asked.

Then Willie came in
with his cat.
"Why are you pulling
that rope with a loop
at the end of it?"
he asked.

"Because there's a dog there,"
said Suzy.

"A dog?" said Willie.
"I don't see any dog."

"That's because
he's invisible
to everyone but me!"

"What does he look like then?"
asked Willie.

"He has big brown eyes
and a long tail," said Suzy.

"Well, why can't I
hear him bark?" asked Willie.

"Because his bark is invisible,
too," said Suzy.

97

Suzy got down on the ground
next to the loop.
"Howard!" she said.
"Don't lick me.
Stop, I say.
All right,
all right.
I'll take you out
for a walk."

Suzy ran out
pulling the rope.

Willie wanted to play
with his cat,
but the cat ran away.
From the window,
Willie could see Suzy
playing with Howard.
Suzy threw an old shoe.
Then she and Howard
ran after the shoe.
"Nice dog," Suzy yelled.

Suzy came back
into the house
pulling Howard's rope.
"Do you want my cat?"
Willie asked.
"I'll give you my cat
for your dog."

"For Howard? Never!"

"Please, Suzy?"
asked Willie again.

"All right,"
Suzy said at last.
"Here is the rope.
Where is the cat?"

"In the other room,"
said Willie.

Willie took the rope
and ran out to play
with Howard.

When he came back,
Suzy was playing
with the cat.
Willie just looked
at them.
Then he called to his dog,
"Stop it, Howard.
Leave the cat alone!"
Willie ran around
the room after Howard.

The cat ran out.

"You scared my cat,"
Suzy yelled at Willie.

"I did not!
The **dog** did!" said Willie.

"I didn't see
any **dog**," Suzy said.

"That's because
the dog is
invisible,"
said Willie.

Suzy and Willie
looked at each other
and began to laugh.

Then Suzy ran out
to get the cat.

"Here, Willie,
it's your turn
to hold **our** cat."

I stand on the rock.
Ho, bear!
Beware of me!

I stand on the tree.
Ho, eagle!
Beware of me!

I stand on the mountain.
Ho, enemy!
Beware of me!

I stand in the camp.
Ho, chiefs!
Beware of me!

Here comes a bee!
I run and hide!
He would sting me!

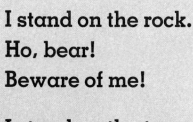

CARMEN
Bill Binzen

It was raining. It was always raining
in New York.

Carmen ran home from school.
She thought, "In Puerto Rico it rains
for a little, and then the sun comes out.
I wish it were like that here!"

 Carmen had just moved to New York from Puerto Rico. She had moved with her family. She missed her home in Puerto Rico. She missed the sun. And she missed her friends, too.

On her way home, Carmen had to buy some potatoes for her mother. She had the money in her pocket.

After she got the potatoes, she came out to the side of the street. There was so much rain water running down the street. Carmen decided to jump over the water. But she couldn't make it, and she fell down right in the water! The potatoes flew all over the street, and Carmen got all wet.

Carmen was happy to get home.
She got out of her wet dress.
She decided to put on
her very nice dress. It would help
to make her happy. She thought
of the day when her mother gave her
the dress, back in Puerto Rico.

"I wish I had something to do,"
Carmen thought. "If only I had
a friend to play with." Her brother
was home, but he was playing
with his new car.

For a long time Carmen sat
in the window and looked down
on the street. She watched
a garbage truck come slowly by.

The garbage collectors walked
behind the truck. They put the garbage
in the back of the truck.

"I wouldn't want to be a garbage collector
in all this rain," Carmen said.

"You wouldn't want to be one
if the sun were out," said her brother.

Then another truck came down the street.

"I wouldn't want to drive a truck
in all this rain," Carmen thought.
But she didn't say it. She didn't want
her brother to hear.

There wasn't much to watch
from the window after that.
There was no one in the street.

Carmen was sad. "Why does it always
have to rain?" she thought. "I wish
there were something to do!" She was
feeling sorry for herself.

107

Just then Carmen saw something!
She saw a little girl with long hair.
She, too, was looking out a window.
She had on a dress very much
like Carmen's and she looked
about as old as Carmen.

Carmen put her hand up, and
the other girl put her hand up, too.
Then Carmen began to feel good
all over. She got her doll and put
it up in the window next to her.

The other girl smiled when she saw
the doll. Then she went away
for a little time. When she came back,
she had a little bear.

Soon the girls were making signs
to each other, and making up
all kinds of silly games.
Time flew by. They forgot
about the rain.

Then, the other girl pointed at Carmen.
Then she pointed down at the street.

"I wonder what she means," Carmen thought,
as the little girl pointed again.

Then Carmen saw that the rain
had stopped. Now she knew what
all that pointing was about. Her new friend
was saying, "I'll see you outside."

"Please, Mother, can I go out?"
Carmen asked. Her mother hardly had
time to say yes before Carmen was
out the door and running down
to the street.

Her friend was waiting!

For a little time the two girls
didn't know what to say.
It was funny being together,
face to face.

"Hello," said the girl. "I'm Liza."

"Hello," said Carmen. "I'm Carmen."

"Let's play a game," said Liza.

"Yes, let's," said Carmen.

They had so much fun together
playing games on the street.

Soon Carmen's mother called,
"Carmen, it's time for you to come
to eat."

"Who wants to eat?" thought Carmen.
But then she smiled and said,
"See you soon, Liza."

Liza smiled. "Yes, I'll see you
soon," she said.

When the next day came, it was raining
again. Rain, rain, rain. But Carmen
didn't care, and Liza didn't care.

This time, they were in one house together. And they were in one window together. And the doll and the bear were right there with them.

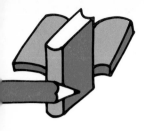

Can You Hear the Sound?

Say each picture name. The blue letters spell a long vowel sound. Listen to that sound when you say the words. Then read the story. Find the words with letters that spell the same long vowel sound. Write the words on your paper.

cake

train

A. Fred had to rake the leaves. But it began to rain. So Fred went in. What could he do? He could make a game. He could paint. He could just wait for the rain to stop, too.

1. rake

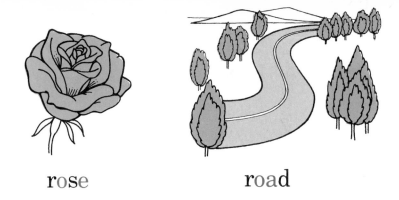

rose road

B. Tom's father went to see his boat. But it was not there. He put on his coat and walked all around the lake. When he found his boat, he took it back home. He tied up the boat with a rope.

queen beans

C. Kim peeked out of the window. She saw the big tree. It had lost its last leaf. The leaf had fallen in the street. Kim thought about how green the tree was in May.

Henry's Pennies

Louise Greep McNamara

Part One
A Lot of Pennies

Henry loved Sundays. Every Sunday, at breakfast, Henry would give his father a special look. And then his father would put his hand in his pocket as Henry watched.

"Let's see how many pennies I have for you today," his father would say.

116

Then he would take out all the pennies
in his pocket and give them to Henry.

Henry had a lot of pennies. He loved to
count them. "One, two, three..." He would
never know just how many he had, so he
counted all of them every Sunday.

People sometimes asked him
what he was going to do with all his pennies.
All he ever said was, "You'll see."
But Henry didn't really know yet.

Sometimes he thought of all the candy
he could buy with his pennies. But then
he would think about the big boys.
What if they took his candy away from him?

And even if the boys didn't take
his candy, his mother would never
let him have it. She always said
too much candy wasn't good for you.
Even if he could find a way to hide
the candy in his room, his baby sister
would be sure to find it.

So Henry just said "You'll see," when
people asked about his pennies.

119

One day at school his friend Chippy said
to him, "Are you going to the fair?"

"What fair?" asked Henry.

"The fair in the school playground
on Friday," said Chippy. "It will be fun.
There will be candy and things to eat.
There will be pony rides and a lot
of old things that you can buy. I know
all about it. My mother is running
the White Elephant Sale."

"A white elephant sale? Zowee!"
said Henry. "Zowee!"

That night Henry asked his mother
if he could go to the fair.
When she said yes, he was so happy
he yelled "Zowee!" again.

When he went to bed, Henry didn't
fall asleep right away. He thought about
what he was going to do with his pennies.
On Friday he would buy a white elephant!

Henry saw himself riding to school
on—on—**Snowdrop!** That's what he would
call her. How happy his mother would be
to have a little white elephant
to clean up the dry leaves!
How happy his father would be to have
a little elephant to take out the garbage!
It made him laugh to think how
Snowdrop could play with his baby sister.

Where would Snowdrop sleep?
The doghouse in back of the house was
too little. But Henry was sure he could find
a place. Henry thought about Snowdrop
for a long time before he fell asleep.

Part Two
Pennies and Peanuts

The morning of the fair came at last.
Henry jumped out of bed fast.
After breakfast he ran to his room.
He put his pennies in his special sock.
He put the sock in his coat pocket
and ran off to school.

At school, everyone asked,
"What do you have in the sock, Henry?"
But he didn't want people to know.
He didn't let go of the sock all morning.

122

But Henry's friend Chippy could hear
the pennies in the sock. "Gee, Henry,"
he said, "you have an awful lot of money
in that sock. You can get a lot of cookies
and candy with all that money."

"I could, couldn't I?" was all Henry said.

Chippy knew about the pennies.
But what he didn't know was that Henry had
put some peanuts in the sock, too.
The peanuts would be a present for Snowdrop.

When school was over for the day,
Henry ran out the door as fast as he could.
And Chippy ran right behind him.

When the boys got to the playground,
they saw balloons and tables.
There were people and food everywhere.
Chippy stopped for a hot dog and
some cookies. But Henry walked on.

"Want to ride a pony?" asked a girl
in a big hat.

"No, thanks," Henry said.
"Could you tell me where
the white elephant sale is?"

"I think it's at the other side
of the playground," said the girl.

Henry was scared that he would be
too late. He began to run. Then he saw
Chippy's mother behind a long table.
She saw Henry at the same time.

"How are you, Henry?" she asked.
"What can I do for you?"

"I'm here to buy it," said Henry.

"Buy what?" asked Chippy's mother.

"You know—the white elephant."

"Well," she said, "we have
a lot of things you can buy. Would you like
this soup spoon? You could give it
to your mother."

"I . . . . ." was all Henry said.

125

"Or this painted donkey? With a new tail,
it would look like new. Or how about
this red ball for your sister?"

"No," said Henry. "What I really want
is the little white elephant. I'm going
to call her Snowdrop. Where is she?"

"Henry," said Chippy's mother,
"we don't have any **real** elephants.
A white elephant is something someone has
and doesn't really want. That's what
all the things you see on the table are.
People who didn't want them gave them to us
for the White Elephant Sale. Other people
will buy them and take them home."

There was no live little white elephant?
Just some old things people didn't want?
Henry wanted to run away. He didn't want
Chippy's mother to see his tears.

Part Three
Snowdrop

Henry was about to leave
the White Elephant Sale. Then he saw
something move on another table.
The thing that moved was in a box
with holes. And it was white.

Henry walked over to see what it was.
There in the box was a very little rabbit!
It was white as snow. Henry put in his hand
to feel the rabbit. It was soft as could be.
It put its nose on Henry's hand.

Chippy's mother was watching. "She has
a collar and leash," she said. "Why don't you
play with her over there on the grass?"

Chippy's mother gave the collar and leash
to Henry. He put them on the rabbit.
Then he took the rabbit out of the box.
"Come on," he said. And she came!
She hopped, hopped, hopped along
right behind Henry. He stopped. She stopped.
Henry laughed. Then he looked at her.

"I think you want something to eat,"
he said. "Some grass, I bet." He thought
of the green grass in back of his house.
And he thought of the doghouse
that no one lived in.

Henry put his hand on her soft back.
He thought of how happy
this soft white rabbit would make
his baby sister. And to think no one wanted
this rabbit!

"Henry," called Chippy. "Wait for me.
Gee, where did you get that rabbit?"

Chippy's mother came up behind them.
"The fair will be over soon, boys," she said.
"Well, Henry, how do you like Snowdrop?"

"Snowdrop? How did you know her name?"
asked Henry.

"It's a very good name for a white rabbit,"
said Chippy's mother.

Slowly Henry asked, "How many pennies for her? I have just three hundred."

"You can have her for two hundred pennies," she said. "And the collar and leash come with her."

Henry counted out two hundred pennies
one by one. Just as he counted out the last
of the pennies, the peanuts fell out
of his sock. Henry cracked one open
and gave it to Snowdrop. She ate it up
and looked at Henry for more.

"She likes peanuts!" he said.
"When I get her home, she can eat grass
most of the time. But sometimes I'll give her
peanuts."

Henry put his hand in his sock.
He still had pennies to buy a balloon
for his baby sister and some cookies
for his mother and father.

Then all the pennies were gone.
Henry put his sock in his pocket.
He made sure he had all his things.

"Come on, Snowdrop," he said.
"Let's go home."

What Goes at the End?

Look at the special sign at the end of this sentence.

What a nice red car Carmen has!

This sentence shows surprise. It has an ! at the end.

Look at the special sign at the end of this sentence.

Have you seen Carmen's new car?

This sentence asks a question. It has a ? at the end.

Look at the special sign at the end of this sentence.

My brother has a car.

This sentence tells something. It has a . at the end.

Read each sentence below. The special
sign is missing from each sentence.
Write each sentence on your paper.
Use the right sign at the end of
each sentence.

1. May we go to the zoo today
2. How I like to go to the zoo
3. The zoo is on Lucky Street

4. The birthday present was on the table
5. What a great birthday present that is
6. Who gave me this birthday present

7. Debbie has a dog
8. Where is Debbie's dog
9. What a great big dog Debbie has

10. Harry eats breakfast every day
11. Did Harry eat breakfast yet
12. What a good breakfast

13. Look how well Winifred rides her bike
14. Can Winifred ride your bike
15. Winifred has a bike

BELIEVE IT

It's not as hard to learn something
new if you believe you can do things.
If you believe in what you can do,
you may find that you can do things
you never thought of doing.

Thinking About "Believe It!"

1. How did the little brown bear find out
   what job he could do best?
2. Why do you think other people didn't
   like the things Winifred made?
3. What kinds of things do people sometimes
   see when they look at clouds?
4. How did Henry find something special
   to buy with his pennies?
5. What kind of job do you think
   you could do best?

FEELINGS

Things that other people do and say can make you feel many ways. If you see someone you like, you feel happy. If someone says something mean, you may feel angry. You have many kinds of feelings. Your feelings are important.

In "Feelings," you will read about a boy who can talk about his feelings. You will read about a crow who feels sad. You will read about a girl who wants to keep too many animals. As you read, look for words that tell you how people feel. Do you sometimes feel the things they feel?

I Have Feelings

Terry Berger

I have feelings.
Some are good and some are bad,
just like yours.

In the spring I put some seeds
in a big flower pot. One day little
green leaves came up from the seeds.
And they grew and grew. By fall,
there were big red beets in the pot.
My mother cut them up and cooked them.

I felt proud.

Every day I watered the seeds and really
took good care of them. I think that's
why the beets were so good. Working
hard at something helps to make it
come about. I felt proud that everyone
liked the beets.

Sometimes my brother makes fun of me when we are at the table. He keeps calling me names. He keeps on making funny faces at me. I feel like yelling back at him.

I feel angry.

After a while I just try not to hear
what he's saying. I try to think about
some other things. He doesn't always
mean the bad things he says about me.
I know this because I sometimes
say bad things about my brother, too.
And I don't really mean them.

On Fridays my mother takes me shopping.
I show her a game that I want.
She will not buy it for me. She says,
"Next time." Or she says, "You have one
just like it."

I feel that my mother does not love me.

As we drive home, I don't say anything
for a while. Then my mother asks me
about school and about my friends. I
tell her all about them. I love talking
to my mother. I know she really cares
for me. I didn't get the game, but no
one can get everything he wants.

Today I tried out for the school band.
I felt awful, but soon I was all right.
I made it!

I felt good!

Now I'm happy that I worked hard to get
into the band. I didn't get to watch some
ball games. And I didn't get to play
with my friends as much as I wanted to.
Sometimes you have to give up something
to get something you want even more.
Our band is going to play on Mother's Day.
My mother says she will come, and I know
she will be so proud of me.

When I get home, Larry calls to tell me that he can't come over. I have no one to play with. I wanted to show him my new kitten.

I feel lonely.

After a while I get a book. It turns out to be a great book with lots of animals in it. Now I know about a fish that walks. Now I know that I can have fun when I am alone, too. With my book I don't feel lonely any more.

It's Friday after school and I have
no homework. Soon I'll be going out
with John, who is lots of fun. We are
going to ride our bikes in the park.
Then we will go fishing at the lake.

I feel happy.

I am happy when I do something I like.

I am happy when I'm with someone I like.

I am happy because I like myself.

Undefeated

A little square of earth
The sidewalk forgot to cover.
 Lost.
 Alone.
Until weeds start coming up.

—Robert Froman

Keep Running, Allen

Clyde Robert Bulla

**Part One
Hurry Up, Allen!**

Allen had a sister and two brothers.

Jenny was the oldest. Then came Mike and Howard. Allen came last.

He was the youngest and the smallest.

Every day they played up and down the street.

Mother told Allen, "Stay with your sister and brothers."

But Jenny and Mike and Howard
went too fast. They had lots of places
to go, and they never stayed anywhere
very long.

By the time Allen caught up with
them, they were off again.

"Hurry up, Allen!" they would call
back to him. "Keep running, Allen!"

One day they heard that the
ice-cream man was giving away free
samples. They ran after the ice-cream
truck.

151

"Run, Allen," said Mike. "Hurry up."

But the ice-cream man wasn't giving away free samples.

They saw old Mr. Feather on his way to mail a letter. "Let's go help him," said Howard.

"Come on, Allen," said Jenny. "Keep running."

She and Mike and Howard helped Mr. Feather mail his letter.

Then Mike said there was a monkey up a tree in the next block. "I think it got out of the zoo," he said.

"Don't stop," Howard called back to Allen. "Hurry up!"

They all ran to the next block. But it wasn't a monkey up the tree. It was only a boy looking for birds' nests.

They chased a big dog. "Maybe it's lost," said Jenny. "If we catch it, we might get a reward."

They chased it as far as the park, and it got away.

All the time Allen had been running after them. He didn't catch up till they stopped at the park.

Then they didn't want to stay.

"Let's go home," said Mike. "I want to get my bike."

"I want to get mine, too," said Howard.

"If we'd had our bikes," said Jenny, "that dog wouldn't have got away."

And the three of them were off again.

Part Two
Allen Stops

Allen was hot and out of breath, but he started after them. He stepped on his shoelace and fell down.

He lay there. The grass felt good.

"Allen!" called Jenny.

"Allen!" called Mike and Howard.

He didn't move. There was a fuzzy green worm in the grass. He wanted to see if it would crawl over his hand. He lay very still, and it did crawl over his hand.

A bluejay scolded him. He waved at it, and it flew away.

He looked at the sky. There were white clouds, and he could see things in them. He saw a funny face—and a chicken—and a woman in a chair.

He heard Jenny say, "*Allen!*"

He heard Mike say, "Where is he?" and Howard said, "There he is."

They had come back.

Jenny said, "What's the *matter* with you? Get up."

He looked at them. He didn't get up.

"Let's just leave him," said Mike.

"We're going to leave you, Allen," said Howard.

"We *can't* leave him," said Jenny. "Get up, Allen."

But he didn't get up.

"Don't be stubborn," said Jenny.

"You look like a big old slug, Allen," said Mike. "This is how you look."

He went limp and flopped down onto the grass. He said, "This is soft."

"What is soft?" asked Howard.

"The grass," said Mike. "It's soft as a bed."

Howard tried it. He lay on his back. "It *is* soft. And it smells like—it smells like *grapes*."

"More like watermelons," said Mike.

"It does not!" said Jenny.

"You can't tell from up there," said Howard.

Jenny lay down. She leaned back.
"Maybe it is a little like grapes. A little
like watermelons, too," she said. "Oh,
look up there! Look at that cloud. It's
a frog."

"Now it's turning into an old shoe," said Mike. "Look up at the sky and shut your eyes a little. Doesn't it make you feel—dreamy?"

They lay there for a while. They stopped talking and just looked at the sky. They all lay in a row, and it was the best time Allen had ever had.

FIELDS

Ann Nolan Clark

Brown fields,
With ground all broken,
I walk softly over you.
I would not hurt you,
While you keep
The baby corn seeds sleeping.

See, brown fields,
The sun will shine for you;
The sun will warm you,
And make you happy.

Soon the rains will come
And wet you,
And give you water
For your baby corn seeds sleeping.
The sun will call the corn seeds;
The rain will call the corn seeds;
They will push up;
Little corn seeds will push up,
Up through the broken ground,
Little corn seeds growing.

Brown fields,
You will turn to green;
Little green corn ears
Growing,

Little green corn ears
Dancing,
For the rain,
For the sun.

A Surprise for Abe

Laurence Swinburne

Part One
The Farm in Indiana

The winter of 1820 was a cold one in Indiana. Snow fell nearly every day. Snow was high around the little farm house where the Lincolns lived. They could feel the wind even inside their house.

Abe Lincoln was just a boy. But he helped Tom, his father, around the farm. He looked after the horse. He milked the cow. He cut wood. But there wasn't much for the Lincoln boys and girls to do for fun.

Abe wanted to go to school. But there was no school in this place.

One night the Lincoln family was sitting by the fire. Mrs. Lincoln looked at Abe.

"Don't look so sad, Abe," said Mrs. Lincoln. "It will be spring soon. Why, it's February now."

"I don't think winter will ever be over," he said. "I hate this place."

Mrs. Lincoln could have cried.
She was so sorry for Abe. The last
three years had been sad for him.
The Lincolns had moved to a farm
in Indiana and the move was hard
on Abe. Then Abe's mother had died.

After a while Abe's father
had found a new wife. She was
a good stepmother to Abe. And she
really loved the boy. She hated
seeing him look so sad all the time.
She tried to think of ways to make him
happy. She wished there was a school
for Abe. But there wasn't, and she
couldn't do anything about it.

The next day she took
all her pennies from a small box.
"I'm going to town," she said.

"Town?" Tom Lincoln said.
He was surprised. "That's a far way.
And the snow is high."

"I'm going," she said.

"What for?" Tom Lincoln asked.

"It's a surprise," she said.

"Do you want Abe or me to come along?" Tom asked his wife.

She shook her head. "I'll be all right," she said, as she went out of the house.

Part Two
Mrs. Lincoln Goes to Town

Tom was right. The snow was high.
It took a long time to get to town.

Mr. Smith looked at Mrs. Lincoln
when she came into his shop.

"What are you doing out?" he cried.
"Your face is all red! You sit right
down and get warm."

He gave her hot milk and food.

"Thank you, Mr. Smith," she said.

"Glad to help you," he said.

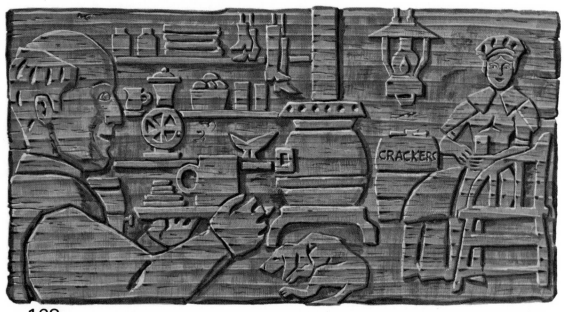

"I came to buy something,"
she said. "That over there."

Mr. Smith looked. "It's not much
good," he said. "I got it from a farmer.
He had it a long time."

"I want it," she said. She gave
him 16 pennies. "It's all I have."

He had given the farmer 14 pennies
for it. He would make only two pennies
on the sale. But Mrs. Lincoln was
a good woman. And she had come
a long way.

"All right," he said. "I'll put
it in a box for you."

Going home was as hard as going
to town. It was very cold.
The snow fell harder than before.

Abe was sleeping when his stepmother
got back.

"What is the surprise?" asked Tom.

"You'll find out in the morning,"
she said as she shook the snow
off her coat.

Part Three
The Surprise

It snowed even harder the next day.
Mrs. Lincoln got up before the sun.
She cooked for a long time. Then Tom
and Abe and the other boys and girls
got out of bed.

Tom and Abe went out for milking.
Everyone had work to do, and the day
went by very fast.

That night everyone sat down
at the table.

"What day is it, Abe?" Mrs. Lincoln asked softly.

"Is it Friday?" he asked.

"It's February 12," she said.

"Oh," he said. It didn't mean much to him.

"It's your birthday!" she cried.

"I forgot," he said. He didn't care. What was a birthday to him? Just another day. He would be a year older, that's all.

"So we are going to have a party!"
she said.

She put food on the table. "Baked
potatoes," she said. "And some fish."

No one said a word. They had had
this food all winter.

"I made a small cake," she said.
She put it on the table. Everyone smiled.
Even Abe smiled, but only a little
and not for long.

"That's not all," she said.
Then she put her present before Abe.

His eyes became very wide.
"A book!" he said. "A book!"

It was an old book. Part of it
was missing. But Abe didn't care.
He began to read the stories.

174

"It's got stories," he cried.
"Lots of stories."

"You like books that much?" asked
Tom. "Even an old book?"

"I want to know what is in books,"
said Abe. "Even an **old** book."

He began to read the stories.
Then Mrs. Lincoln got the present she
had waited for all winter. The present
was the smile on Abe's face.

A Hat Goes on a Head

Read each sentence below. The last
word in each sentence is missing.
Choose a word to finish the sentence.
Write the sentence on your paper.
Fill in the missing word.

1. Just as a <u>hat</u> goes on a <u>head,</u>
   a <u>shoe</u> goes on a ____.
        back   hand   foot

   1. Just as a hat goes on a head,
      a shoe goes on a foot.

2. Just as a <u>bird</u> can <u>fly,</u>
   a <u>fish</u> can ____.
        walk   swim   bark

3. Just as an <u>elephant</u> is very <u>big,</u>
   a <u>mouse</u> is very ____.
        cold   high   little

4. Just as you <u>sleep</u> in a <u>bed</u>,
you <u>sit</u> in a ____.
   table   chair   garbage

5. Just as the <u>grass</u> is <u>green</u>,
the <u>sky</u> is ____.
   blue   yellow   brown

6. Just as Joshua <u>laughs</u> when he is <u>happy</u>,
he <u>cries</u> when he is ____.
   sad   strong   proud

7. Just as your <u>nose</u> is part of your <u>face</u>,
your <u>finger</u> is part of your ____.
   head   hand   foot

8. Just as <u>boats</u> move on the <u>water</u>,
<u>cars</u> move on the ____.
   sky   lake   land

177

The Magic Alligator

Richard E. Martin

One day a bear and a dog and a rabbit and a crow went off to the swamp. They wanted to call on the magic alligator.

They had never seen the magic alligator. But they knew all about him. It was said that he could help anyone who had a special problem. And the crow had a very special problem. He thought no one liked him.

So the bear and the dog and the rabbit were taking him to the magic alligator. The crow needed help.

The bear and the dog and the rabbit really liked the crow. But they didn't like the way he flew around all day screaming, "No one likes me! No one likes me!"

"I've had it," the rabbit said one day. "I can't put up with any more of his screaming."

So they decided to take the crow to the magic alligator. On the way to the swamp, the crow flew over the heads of the others. He screamed "No one likes me! People put up scarecrows to keep me away. No one likes me!"

NO ONE LIKES ME
NO ONE LIKES ME

The bear and the dog and the rabbit went on. They went on into the swamp.

"I'll bet he's around here," said the bear.

"Maybe he's in the water," said the dog.

"What's that in the tree?" asked the rabbit.

"It's a magic alligator if I ever saw one," said the crow. He had never seen any kind of alligator until then. "And he doesn't like me," he said.

180

The alligator was fast asleep
on the branch of a tree.
It was ten feet from the ground.

"Hello, magic alligator," called
the dog.

The alligator opened one eye. He
said, "Hello. Did you come for lunch?"

"No," said the rabbit. "We have
a friend with us. He has a very special
problem. We want you to help him.
Crow, here, thinks no one likes him."

"Is he fat?" asked the alligator.

"Yes, he's fat," said the bear.

"Good," said the alligator. "Tell him to come up!"

"O.K., crow, get up there," said the dog. "He'll make everyone like you."

"All right," said the crow. He went flying up to the magic alligator.

"Now," said the magic alligator, "turn around and don't look at me. Just think I'm working my magic on you."

As soon as the crow had turned his back, the alligator ate him up.

"What are you doing to old crow?" cried the bear.

"Give us back our crow," yelled the dog.

"Quick, bear! Get that alligator," said the rabbit.

The bear got the magic alligator by the tail and pulled. Down came the alligator from the tree.

"Make him give us back our crow," said the rabbit. "Jump on his back, bear."

The bear jumped on his back. But the alligator just laughed.

"Jump on him again," said the dog. **"Harder."**

The bear jumped on him again. The alligator's eyes got big.

"One more time," said the rabbit.

The bear jumped high in the air and landed hard on the alligator.

"P--oof!" said the alligator, and out flew the crow.

"Let's get out of here," said
the rabbit.

As they were leaving the swamp,
the crow flew ahead of the others.
He said, "You like me! You like me!"

The bear and the dog and
the rabbit knew things would be
quieter in the woods now. But they
were still not sure about the alligator.
Was he magic or wasn't he?

YOU LIKE ME— YOU LIKE ME—

BE CAREFUL!

If you should meet a crocodile,
   Don't take a stick and poke him;
Ignore the welcome in his smile,
   Be careful not to stroke him.
For as he sleeps upon the Nile,
   He thinner gets and thinner;
And whene'er you meet a crocodile
   He's ready for his dinner.

—Anonymous

Friendly (but hungry) Crocodile

LISTEN!

Gina Ingoglia Weiner

Have you ever thought that something in the air has a lot to do with how you feel? You cannot see it, but it's always there. It is sound. Do you know how you hear sound?

You hear sound with your ears. When something makes a sound, the air around it moves in a special way. This moving air is called sound waves. The sound waves go into the hole in your ear. Behind the hole there is a part of your ear called the eardrum. The sound waves hit your eardrum. Then you hear the sound.

There are many kinds of sounds.
If you are at home, you may be listening
to music. Some music is soft and slow.
This kind of music makes you feel
like resting. But what if you hear loud
parade music with drums? Do you still
feel like resting? No! You feel full
of energy. You may want to get right up
and march around the room.

When you go to a parade, it's fun
to watch the people marching. But it
would not be as much fun without
the parade music. It's the sound
of the music and the drums that makes
you feel like marching, too.

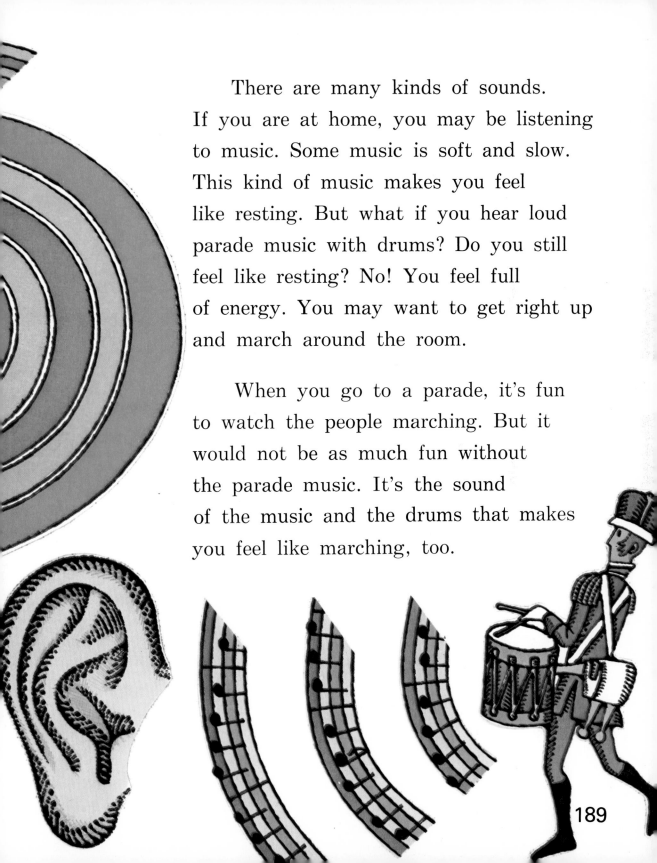

It's nice to hear the sound of rain falling on your window at night. You feel happy that you are in a dry, warm house. But then—BOOM! There is the cracking sound of thunder. Thunder could never hurt you. But it still makes you jump and feel scared.

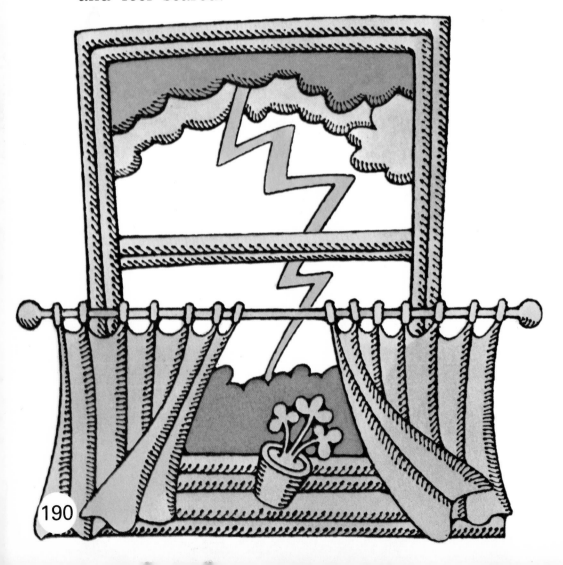

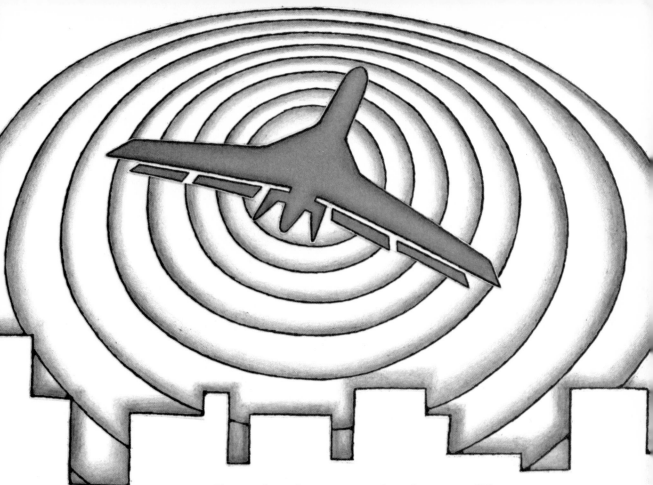

Sounds that people do not like
to hear are called noise. You hear
noise when a great jet is taking off.
You hear noise in city streets. You
hear noise when a fire truck goes by.

Noise can make you want
to hold your ears. Some noise
can be scary. Your ears may even hurt
if there is too much noise.

There is a soft, street sound
that you like to hear. It's the bell
on the ice-cream truck. You wish that
your mother would let you have some.
You're sad if she says, "No." And you're
happy if she says, "Yes." Isn't it funny
that this little bell makes you
have so many feelings?

You have feelings when there is
very little sound, too. At rest time
in school it's very quiet. You may
feel like resting because everything
is so still. But you may feel like
making a lot of noise. You may think
it's much too quiet!

ICE CREAM

Sometimes one sound can make you feel happy and sad in the same day. You have asked a friend over to your house. You're happy when you hear the doorbell. It means your friend has come. But, in a little while, you hear the doorbell again. You're sad. You know your friend's father has come to take your friend home. The sound of the doorbell has made you happy *and* sad all in one day!

Sounds are everywhere. They are in the quiet country. They are on city streets. They are in your house and in your room. There is always something for you to hear. Listen!

193

I Hear

Night Sounds

When I go to bed
I hear my brother
Talking to me
I hear the TV
I hear the branches
Clicking at the window
I hear the lights
Clicking on and off
I hear my mom and dad
Talking
I hear my sister
Come in late at night
I hear cars
Roaring down our street.
Good night!

by Terry

I Hear

Day Sounds

When I play I hear
Roller skates on the sidewalk
And a bird chirping
And the wind whispering
And the trees rustling
And the swings creaking.

by Laura

The sound poems were made by a boy
and a girl about your age. Do you
hear the same day sounds?
Do you hear the same night sounds?
What other sounds do you hear?
What sounds make you feel happy?
You can make your own sound poem.
Just listen—then write!

One Pet Too Many

Nina B. Link

Part One
A Zoo in One Room

Isabel saw a kitten on the side
of the street. It was sitting
under a blue car.

"Come here, little kitten," Isabel said.
The kitten looked up at Isabel
with big yellow eyes. When Isabel took
her from under the car, she saw
that her leg was hurt.

"I will take care of you," Isabel said
as she put her hand in her soft, black
fur. "You can come home with me."

The kitten gave out a happy cry.

"I'm going to call you 'Fluff' because you are so soft," Isabel said.

Isabel ran all the way home. She had to carry the kitten in one hand and her books in the other. She stopped when she got to the door. She put Fluff into her coat.

As soon as Isabel rang the bell,
her mother was at the door. She
gave Isabel a big hug. Fluff gave
out a little cry.

"I'll be right back," Isabel said
to her mother. "Let me put my
books away."

Isabel ran to her room. She found
an old shoe box. "There you are, Fluff.
You have a home. And there are lots
of friends for you here, too."

With the kitten in her hand, she went around to show Fluff to the other animals in the room.

"This is Pili, the bird," Isabel said. "His wing was hurt, but soon he'll be fine. This is S, the snake. Don't get too close to him until he gets to know you. Look, Micifus! I have found a new friend for you. And..."

Isabel didn't hear the door open as she was showing Fluff to all her other pets.

"Isabel," her mother called out.

Isabel turned around. Her mother looked very angry.

"Now **what** did you carry into this house?" her mother asked.

Isabel showed her mother the kitten.

"This is the end, Isabel. I know you love to take care of animals, but there is just no room. And I have to buy their food, too."

"Just one more kitten won't hurt," Isabel said.

Just then her sister came in. She saw Fluff and gave out a yell. "No more animals in this room! This is my room, too. Mama, I feel like I'm living in a zoo. No one I know has to sleep with cats, dogs, birds, a mouse, a snake, fish, and three turtles. The next thing I know, Isabel will come home with an elephant."

200

"There are other people in the family
to think of, Isabel," her mother said.
"I will give you a few days to find
a place for the animals."

"Can't I keep **any** of my pets?"
Isabel asked.

"You can pick any two," her mother said.

"You had better not keep the snake or
the mouse," her sister yelled as she went
out of the room.

"I know how you feel, Isabel,"
her mother said. "When you grow up,
you can have all the pets you want."

"It takes a long time to grow up,"
Isabel said.

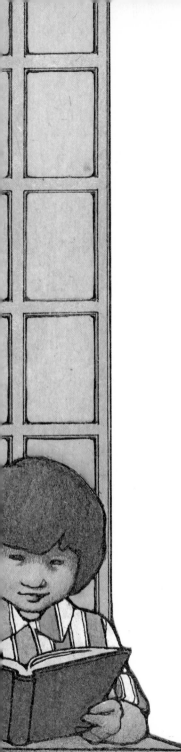

Part Two
A Dog-Walker

For the rest of the day Isabel thought
and thought. She didn't know what
she was going to do with all her pets.
Some she could give to her friends.
Some she would have to let go.
What two pets should she keep?

"I have to keep you, Fluff, because
you are too little to take care
of yourself. And I have to keep Timi,
the dog. No one will want her because
she is so old. She can't even see well
any more."

The next day in school she asked
her friends if they wanted any
of her pets. They didn't.

Isabel felt sad on her way home.
When she saw her father, she said,
"I don't know what to do with my pets.
No one at school wants them."

Father was sorry to see her so sad.
"Isabel, I think I know a way you can
keep all your animals. I'm sure there
is room in the garage if I throw
a few things away," he said.

"Really, Papa? Oh, thank you!" said
Isabel, hugging her father. "Papa,
let's go and make room right now."

Soon, Isabel and her father were
cleaning out the garage. They threw out
some old paint cans. They threw out
Isabel's baby bike. They threw out
some wood that was old and cracked.

Now there was room for her pets
on one side of the garage.

Isabel took Pili, the bird, and S, the snake,
into the garage. She took the fish and
the turtles, too. Her cats, Micifus
and Fluff, came into the garage
after her. Isabel sat down with all
her pets and told them about
their new home. Then it was time
to feed them. She saw that there
wasn't very much food in the box.

Later that day Isabel took her dog Timi for a walk. As she walked, she couldn't help thinking, "I have got to find a way to make some money. I can't keep asking Mama to buy food for my pets."

Just then, the woman next door came up to her with a dog. "Isabel, do you think you can walk my dog today? I have this new job, and now I have hardly any time for my dog," said the woman. "I'll give you a dime."

"Yes, I can walk your dog every day, if you want. I love dogs," said Isabel, all in one breath. She knew how she was going to make money now. She would be a dog-walker!

Isabel went around to every house on her street. In no time she had three dogs to walk every day. Now she could keep all her pets and feed them, too.

The Furry Ones

I like
the furry ones—
the waggy ones
the purry ones
the hoppy ones
that hurry,

The glossy ones
the saucy ones
the sleepy ones
the leapy ones
the mousy ones
that scurry,

The snuggly ones
the hug-ly ones
the never, never
ugly ones...
all soft
and warm
and furry.

—Aileen Fisher

The Little Boy and the Birthdays

Helen E. Buckley

Part One
Birthdays to Remember

Once there was a little boy. He lived with his mother and father and grandmother. One day he was thinking about his birthday. It was a long time away. But he was thinking about it anyway.

"What if no one remembers my birthday?" he said to his mother. "Shall I tell them?"

"No," said his mother. "The best part about birthdays is having people remember without telling them."

"But they would be sorry if they forgot," said the little boy.

"Yes, they would," said his mother. "And so would you. But still the best part about birthdays is having people remember."

"Grandma is getting old," said the little boy. "Will she know about my birthday?"

"No one is ever too old to know about birthdays," said his mother.

"What about Aunty?" asked the little boy. "She lives so far away. Will she remember?"

"No one is ever too far away for birthdays," said his mother.

"But Daddy—what if he is too busy?"

"No one is ever too busy to remember birthdays," said his mother.

"Well, he might," said the little boy.
"Maybe we could put a circle
on the calendar. That wouldn't be
the same as telling."

"We could do that," said his mother.
She went to the calendar on the wall.
Then she put a big circle
around his birthday.

"Now, tell me," she said to him.
"Do you know when Grandma's birthday is,
or Aunty's, or Daddy's?"

"No," said the little boy. "I am
too little to remember."

"But if you can remember
your own birthday, then you are not
too little to remember others, are you?"

212

"No, but we had better put
a circle around them," said the little boy.

"All right," said his mother. And
she made circles around all the days.

"But, when is *your* birthday?" asked
the little boy.

"I'm glad you asked," said his mother.
"Because my birthday is next week!" And
she put another circle on the calendar.

The little boy looked at all
the circles. "My birthday comes last,"
he said. "It's a long time to wait."

"You will be busy remembering
other people's birthdays. It won't seem
long," said his mother.

213

Part Two
You Remembered!

The little boy watched the calendar.
The very next week his mother's
birthday came along. He gave her
a pretty box. In it were two flowers,
a shell, and a tiny horse. He made
a birthday card, too.

"You remembered!" said his mother.
She gave him a special birthday hug.
And the little boy was very pleased.

Then his grandmother's birthday came along. He gave her two pretty little rocks and a birthday card.

"Imagine you remembering my birthday!" said his grandma. "Just imagine!" And she gave him a special grandma hug.

And the little boy was very pleased.

Then his aunty's birthday came along.
He sent her his drawing of a flower and
a birthday card. And what do you think!
His aunty called him to thank him.

"You remembered my birthday," she said.
"I thought I was so far away you would forget."

And the little boy was very pleased.

Then his daddy's birthday came along.
The little boy gave him a clay dog and
a card he had made.

"Well, well!" said his father. "I've
been so busy that I forgot my own birthday.
But you remembered." And he gave
the little boy a piggyback ride.

And the little boy was very pleased.

Now all this time the little boy's birthday was getting closer and closer. He had been so busy that he thought his own birthday was a long time off.

Then one morning, the little boy saw four boxes at the foot of his bed. They had not been there the night before. All of the four boxes had pretty paper on them. Now he knew what day it was.

He ran to the door to call his mother. But, when he opened it, there she was— with his father and his grandma—and his aunty!

"You remembered my birthday!" he cried. He danced up and down. "Imagine that!" And he gave each of them a special birthday kiss. Then he opened his presents.

What Does the Word Mean?

Read each story below. Think about the meaning of the underlined word. Write the sentence with the word meaning on your paper.

An <u>elk</u> is a very big deer. It lives in the woods. An <u>elk</u> eats leaves and grass.

1. An <u>elk</u> is _____.

    an animal

    a car

    a cow

    1. An elk is an animal.

Kim plays the <u>fiddle.</u> People listen to the music she plays. People dance to the music of her <u>fiddle.</u>

2. A <u>fiddle</u> is _____.

    used to make breakfast

    something to write with

    played to make music

A refrigerator keeps food cold and fresh. Milk, eggs, and fish are put in the refrigerator until they are needed.

3. A refrigerator is used ＿＿.

    to hold shoes
    to keep food
    to watch a show

A daffodil is pretty. Most daffodils are yellow. They bloom in the spring.

4. A daffodil is ＿＿.

    a yellow spring flower
    a fast red car
    a happy yellow dog

Carmen and Fred stayed under the shelter when it was raining. The shelter helped them keep dry.

5. A shelter is ＿＿.

    a blue rock
    like a house
    something to read

Beatrix Potter

Elizabeth Levy

Part One
A Lonely Girl

When Beatrix Potter was
a little girl, most little girls did not
go to school. Some little girls
were lucky. They went to school and
made friends. But Beatrix Potter
was not so lucky. Her mother and
father did not think that little girls
needed to go to school. So Beatrix
had no friends.

Beatrix's brother went away to school. But Beatrix stayed home. Most of the time she was alone in her room. Beatrix learned to read and to do many other things. But she had no one to play with.

She had a lot of time to be by herself. So she learned to keep herself happy by making up stories. Sometimes she would make paintings for her stories.

Beatrix loved the summer best of all. Her brother came home from school. And then the Potter family went to the country. All summer Beatrix had someone to play with.

Beatrix and her brother loved the outdoors. They would stop to watch a frog in the lake. They would sometimes stop to see a woodmouse making a house.

One summer Beatrix and her brother decided to make a collection of plants and animals. But they had to hide their collection from their mother. She would have been disgusted at bugs and snakes in her house.

Over the summer Beatrix and her brother made paintings of their collection. They made paintings of rabbits and crows, farms and flowers.

Most of the time Beatrix tried to paint the animals and plants the way they really looked. But sometimes she would paint a mouse with a little hat on. Or she would paint a rabbit with a basket—just like in her stories.

Soon the summer was over. Her brother was back at school. But Beatrix was not as alone as she had been. She became friends with a rabbit called Peter. She had found him in the country. Beatrix's mother did not want Peter Rabbit in the house. But Beatrix found ways to keep him in her room.

Beatrix grew up to be a very quiet young woman. But she had become someone who knew and thought a lot about plants and animals. She had also become someone who knew how to draw.

Part Two
From Scientist to *Peter Rabbit*

The Potter family had a lot of
money. So Beatrix did not need to work.
Her mother and father would not have
liked it anyway. Beatrix's collection
of plant drawings grew. She began
to think that they should be made
into a book. Then scientists
could look at them.

Her mother and father did not think
this was a good idea for a young woman.
But Beatrix had an uncle who thought
that it was a very good idea. He took
her to meet some scientists.

The scientists were not very nice. "She's too young!" they said. "She has not been to school," "She is a girl!" they said. Beatrix's uncle was very angry at the scientists.

"They are silly," he said to Beatrix. "You know as much as they do. Your drawings are better than theirs."

Her uncle told Beatrix to write about one kind of plant. Then he took the paper and had it read before a meeting of scientists. Beatrix could not read the paper herself. She couldn't even go to the meeting. Women were not let into the meetings of the scientists.

Maybe Beatrix could have found a way to be a scientist. Some women did. But Beatrix gave up the idea because her mother and father did not like it.

Beatrix was not really unhappy. She had learned to like being alone. She still painted plants and animals all the time. And she still had old Peter Rabbit. She was happy when she could go away to the country.

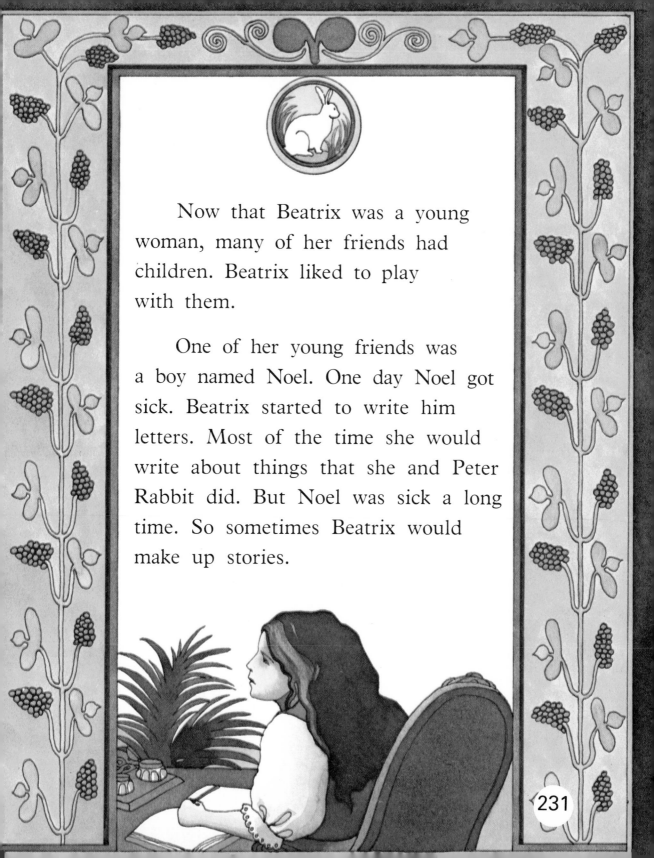

Now that Beatrix was a young woman, many of her friends had children. Beatrix liked to play with them.

One of her young friends was a boy named Noel. One day Noel got sick. Beatrix started to write him letters. Most of the time she would write about things that she and Peter Rabbit did. But Noel was sick a long time. So sometimes Beatrix would make up stories.

Eastwood Dunkeld
Sep 4ᵗʰ 93

My dear Noel,
    I don't know what to write to you, so I shall tell you a story about four little rabbits whose

Flopsy, Mopsy Cotto

, lived with their d bank under th fir tree.

'Now my dears', said old Mrs Bunny 'you may go into the field or down the lane, but don't go into Mr McGregor's garden.'

Flopsy, Mopsy & Cottontail, who were good little rabbits went down the lane to gather blackberries. but Peter, who was very naughty

232

Noel loved her letters. He showed them to all his friends. Everyone loved the story of Peter Rabbit. So Beatrix thought it would be a good idea to have it made into a book.

Peter Rabbit became one of the best-loved children's books of all time. You can tell the drawings were done by someone who knew all about animals. And maybe you can also tell they were done by someone who learned to love little animals because they were her only friends.

THE BREMEN TOWN MUSICIANS

Adapted by **John Ralph**

The Players

Donkey	Robber One
Dog	Robber Two
Cat	Robber Three
Rooster	Storyteller

ACT ONE

Storyteller: Once upon a time there was an old donkey who had worked hard all his life. But now he was old and tired, and his master didn't want him. One morning, before his master was up, the donkey started out for Bremen. It was a town where he had been many times. On his way he came to a river. After he had some cold water, he lay down to rest. Then a big old hunting dog joined him.

Dog: *(Out of breath)* Good morning!

Donkey: Good morning! Where is your master?

Dog: I'm running away from him.

Donkey: That's funny. I'm running away from mine. For many years, it's been nothing but work, work, work! Now that I'm getting old and tired, he doesn't want me.

Dog: I know what you mean. I have been hunting with my master all my life. Now that I'm getting old, he doesn't want me.

Donkey: Where are you going?

Dog: I'm running away. Where are you going?

Donkey: I'm going to Bremen. I have always liked the music of the Bremen street bands. I thought I might join one of them. I still have a pretty good voice. Why don't you join me?

Dog: I don't have a good ear for music.

Donkey: You could play a drum with your tail.

(A cat stops by.)

Donkey: You have a very sad face this morning. What's the matter?

Cat: I have been treated badly by someone I thought loved me. I'm running away.

Donkey: So are we. Why are you running away?

Cat: I'm getting old, and I'm no good at catching mice any more. My master gave a boy money to take me. But I got away.

BREMEN

Donkey: Dog and I are going to try our luck in Bremen, with a street band. Why don't you join us?

Cat: That seems like a good idea. I'm very proud of my voice.

Dog: All right. Let's go.

(A crowing rooster comes flying down the road.)

Rooster: Help! Help! She is after me.

Donkey and Dog: Who is after you?

Rooster: The farmer's wife! She hates my crowing. She is going to make soup out of me.

Donkey: Dog and Cat and I are going to Bremen to join a street band. Maybe we could use your cock-a-doodle-doo here and there.

Rooster: I knew my voice would come in handy some day.

Dog: If we don't get going, we'll never get to Bremen. Come on.

(The animals get up and start down the road.)

ACT TWO

Storyteller: And so the would-be musicians started the long walk to Bremen. They were still a long way from the town when night began to fall. They were so tired that they decided to sleep in the woods. When they were getting ready to sleep, they saw a tiny light at the other end of the woods. They decided to go and see what it was. It could be a house where they might find food and a warm place to sleep. They got nearer and nearer until they were a few feet from an open window. They could hear voices. Donkey went over and looked in the window.

Donkey: There are three men—they look like robbers. They are sitting around the table eating. I have never seen so much food!

Dog: How can we get some of it?

Donkey: We'll go over to the window. Dog will get on my back. Cat will get on Dog, and Rooster will get on Cat. When I give the word, we'll start to sing. The robbers will be so pleased with our music that they will ask us in.

(The animals get on top of each other.)

Donkey: One, two, three!

(The animals sing at the top of their voices. The window breaks, and there is much noise.)

Robber One: *(Yelling)* What on earth is that?

(He runs to the window.)

Robber Two: What is it?

Robber Three: I don't know, but I'm getting out of here. And fast! *(He runs out the door and the others run out after him.)*

Donkey: Well, I don't think they liked our music. Let's go inside.

(They all go inside.)

Dog and Donkey: Look at all that food! Let's eat.

(They sit around the table and begin to eat.)

ACT THREE

Storyteller: Later that night the robbers came back. The animals were sound asleep. The house was dark, and one of the robbers went in to look around. They were not about to give up their house for a little scare. Everything was quiet—until he went to the fire to get a light. The cat, who had been sleeping by the fire, got up at once.

Cat: *(Flying at the robber)* **P-F-S-S-T!**

Robber One: What's that? I can't see. Help! *(He runs to the door, holding his hands to his eyes.)*

Dog: *(At the door)* **GR-R-R-R. GR-R-R-R.** *(Dog bites the robber on the leg. The robber runs out of the house screaming.)*

Robber One: Thank goodness, I got out of—
(*Donkey waits outside the door and gives the robber a hard kick on his back.*) **OUCH !**

Rooster: (*Flying down on the robber with his wings open*) **Cock-a-doodle-doo! Cock-a-doodle-doo!**

Robber One: **Help! Help! Help!** (*He runs for his life until he sees the other robbers.*)

Robber Two: What's the matter?

Robber One: It was awful. The place is full of giants—or something! They bite, they kick, and they scream. I'm bleeding and hurting all over. Oh, you would never get me into that house again.

Robber Three: It's our house. They can't put us out of our own house.

Robber One: Oh, yes, they can. This robber won't try to take it from them. And I don't think you would.

246

Storyteller: So, the robbers went away
and were never seen around there again.
As for the four musicians, they liked
their new house so well that they never
went to Bremen.

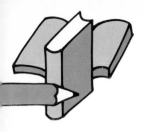

Find the Missing Letters

Look at each picture. Then look at
the word that names the picture.
Choose the letters that will make
the word correct. Write the word on
your paper.

1. f a r m

    ar er

2. ch _ _ _

    air ure

3. flow _ _ _

    er ir

4. n _ _ _ se

    ar ur

5. liz _ _ d

    ir ar

6. c _ _ _ cle

    ir ar

B. One word in each sentence has missing letters. Choose the missing letters that will finish the word. Then write each sentence on your paper with the correct word.

7. A calend＿＿ tells you what day it is.
          ir ar

   7. A calendar tells you what day it is.

8. James turned the wat＿＿ on.
                    er or

9. A g＿＿l played with a dog in a yard.
    ir ar

10. Ann's new cat has such nice f＿＿ .
                    ar ur

11. The g＿＿bage can was turned over.
    ir ar

12. He sc＿＿ed me when he said, "Boo!"
    ar or

13. Andy hurt his fing＿＿playing ball.
      ar er

TARO and the BAMBOO SHOOT

Masako Matsuno

Part One
The Forest

Many years ago, a boy called Taro lived in Japan. He lived in a small village up in the hills. A great forest of bamboo trees grew around the village. It stood like a green wall. It cut off the village from every other place.

Once there had been a path from the village to the far-off sea. But little by little the forest had grown up all over the path. The people had become scared to leave the village. They didn't want to get lost in the great forest. So for years no one had gone away from the village. No one had seen the far-off sea.

Life in the village was very quiet until the day Taro became seven years old. On his birthday Taro's mother said, "Taro, go and dig up a bamboo shoot. I'll make you something special to eat."

So Taro went into the woods just behind his house. He found a nice little bamboo shoot. He started to dig it up. After a while he became very hot. So he took off his coat and put it over another little bamboo shoot.

But right away the little bamboo shoot
started growing very fast. Up, up, up
it went. And Taro's coat went up with it.

"My coat," yelled Taro. He jumped up
to get it. But the shoot grew faster still.
So Taro climbed up the shoot after his coat.
The faster he climbed the faster it grew.
Soon Taro had climbed very, very high.
He was so high he was scared
to look down. Taro's mother came
to look for him.

"Taro-o-o, Taro-o-o," she called.
"Here," came a voice from way up.
Then Taro's mother saw the bamboo shoot
growing up before her very eyes.

"Help, help!" she cried. Taro's father and all the people in the village came running.

"Taro-o-o!" they called up.

"Here," called down Taro. But the people could hardly hear what he said.

"Let's cut down the shoot," said Taro's
father. So the people started to cut away
at the trunk of the bamboo shoot. But
it was no use. The more they cut, the more
the trunk grew. But then, all at once,
the bamboo shoot stopped growing.
It decided to take a rest.

At last the people cut through
the giant trunk.

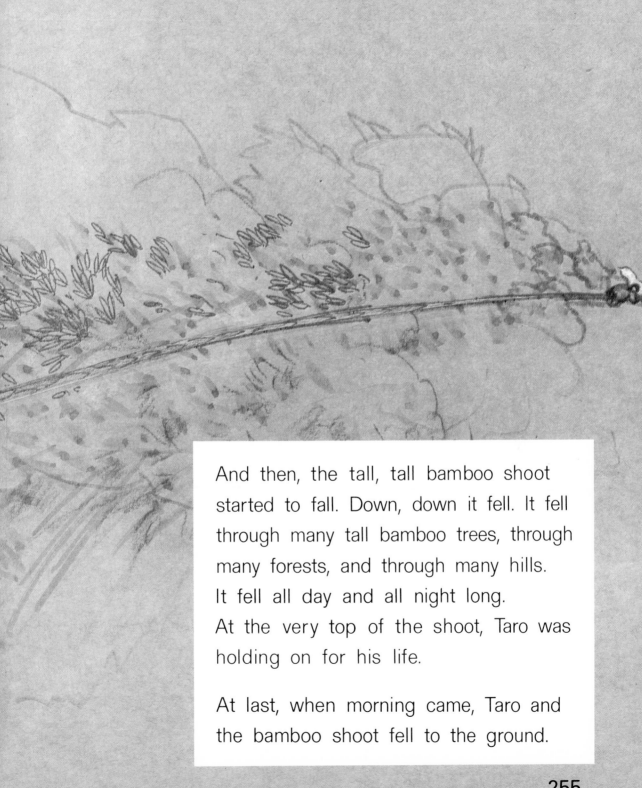

And then, the tall, tall bamboo shoot
started to fall. Down, down it fell. It fell
through many tall bamboo trees, through
many forests, and through many hills.
It fell all day and all night long.
At the very top of the shoot, Taro was
holding on for his life.

At last, when morning came, Taro and
the bamboo shoot fell to the ground.

Part Two
The Sea

Back in the village all the people were watching the bamboo shoot fall. When they saw the great trunk fall to the ground, they all ran ahead. They used the bamboo shoot as a path. They ran along on the bamboo shoot. They ran through many tall bamboo trees, through many forests, and through many hills. At last they came to a great stretch of sand. White sand was all around them. And there was a lake. It stretched as far as they could see.

And there on the sand lay Taro—very still.

Taro's mother ran to the lake. She got some water. She threw it on Taro's face. Everyone cried for joy to see Taro sit up. Taro stretched his arms. Then he said, "Could you stop crying? Your tears are very salty."

"Those are not tears but water from the lake," said Taro's mother.

"Salty lake water? How can it be?" said Taro's father. He ran to the lake to taste the water.

"It is salty," he cried. "This must be the sea!"

"Do you mean the sea that is full of fish?" asked Taro's mother.

"Yes," cried Taro's father. "And seaweed, too. No one in our village has been to the sea in over a hundred years. But from now on, we can come here any time we like. We can use the bamboo shoot as our path."

"Show me some seaweed," cried Taro. "And can you really eat fish?"

"Let's catch some and find out," said
Taro's father.

So some people made fishing poles.
They climbed up on a big rock and fished.
Other people walked along the water looking
for seaweed. Soon they had as much fish
and seaweed as they could carry. Then
everyone started home along the bamboo
shoot path. They walked through many hills,

through many forests, and through many
tall bamboo trees. At last they got back
to their village.

The next night, everyone came to a big
party for Taro's birthday. They ate lots
of fish and seaweed and bamboo shoots.
Everyone said that it tasted much better
than bamboo shoots alone.

After that, the people went to the sea many
times. They would come back with as
much fish and seaweed as they wanted.

Taro and his friends went along to help.
But sometimes Taro would just sit
on the sand. He would look out
over the sea and think about faraway places.

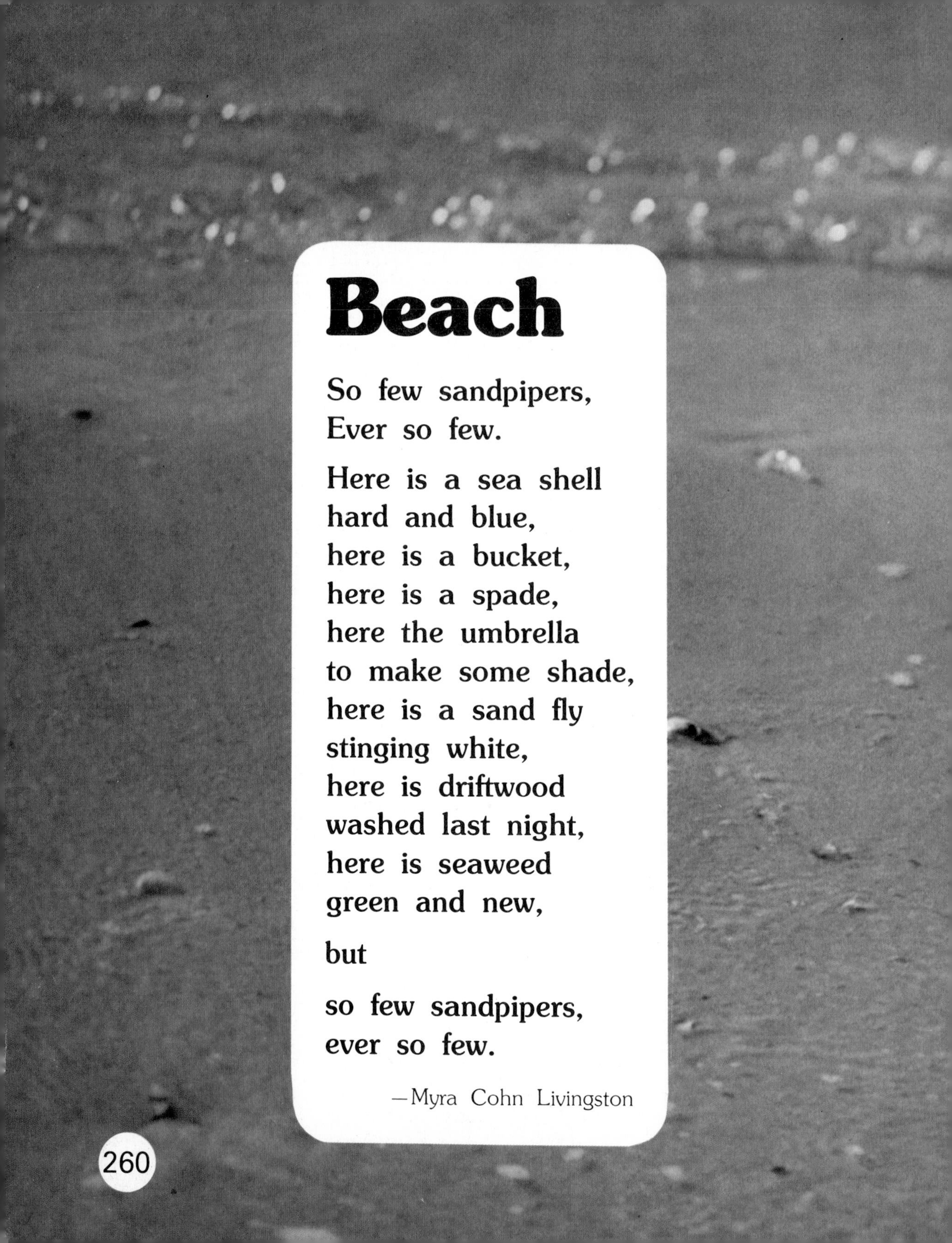

Beach

So few sandpipers,
Ever so few.

Here is a sea shell
hard and blue,
here is a bucket,
here is a spade,
here the umbrella
to make some shade,
here is a sand fly
stinging white,
here is driftwood
washed last night,
here is seaweed
green and new,

but

so few sandpipers,
ever so few.

—Myra Cohn Livingston

What's the Order?

Look at each group of words below.
Write each group of words in
alphabetical order on your paper.

1. red
   eye
   good
   you

1. eye
  good
  red
  you

2. idea
   love
   boat
   mail

3. Winifred
   Sam
   Alice
   Jay

4. umbrella
   air
   turtle
   water

5. queen
   tree
   yard
   color

6. music
   village
   king
   once

7. zoo
   garage
   hair
   night

All the words in each group begin with the *same* letter. Look at the *second* letter in each word. Then write the words in alphabetical order on your paper.

8. boy
blue
bugs
break

8. blue
boy
break
bugs

9. present
pick
party
place

10. dragon
did
dog
day

11. rock
rabbit
run
real

12. fog
frog
flower
face

13. ask
awful
all
angry

14. humming
horse
happy
hill

FEELINGS

All people have feelings. In "Feelings,"
you read about the ways some people felt.
The same things don't always make people
feel the same way.

Thinking About "Feelings"

1. How do you think Allen felt about
   the things Jenny, Mike, and Howard
   liked to do?
2. Why did the rabbit, the bear, and
   the dog want to help the crow?
3. How did Isabel's sister feel about
   the animals that Isabel liked?
4. Why did Beatrix Potter learn to
   love animals so much?
5. When you see your friends, how can
   you tell what your friends are
   feeling?

Glossary

A

a · bove   The bird flew <u>above</u> the house.

a · head   Ann ran <u>ahead</u> of the others, and I stayed behind.

air   Music filled the <u>air</u>.

al · li · ga · tor   The <u>alligator</u> swam in the river.

al · most   Betsy is <u>almost</u> seven years old.

an · gry   Rosa was <u>angry</u> because she got paint on her new dress.

a · sleep   Be very quiet and the baby will fall <u>asleep</u>.

B

bal · loons   I blew up two red <u>balloons</u> for the party.

bam · boo   The fishing pole was made of <u>bamboo</u>.

bang   The door closed with a <u>bang</u>.

bark   My dog will <u>bark</u> when it wants to eat. Its <u>bark</u> is loud.

be · cause   I gave her a present <u>because</u> it is her birthday.

been   The ground is wet because it has <u>been</u> raining all day.

be · fore   The bird flew away <u>before</u> the cat could catch it.

be · gin   If we <u>begin</u> to work now, we will be done at the end of the day.

be · hind   If we hide <u>behind</u> the tree, no one will see us.

bet · ter   We had <u>better</u> leave now or we will be late for school.

birds'   The <u>birds'</u> wings moved slowly.

266

blew   I <u>blew</u> up a balloon last night.

block   Allen likes to play with other children on his <u>block</u>.

blow   Today I can <u>blow</u> up two balloons.

boom   We heard the <u>boom</u> of the thunder.

bot • tom   We ran down to the <u>bottom</u> of the hill.

bright   The sun was so <u>bright</u> that it hurt my eyes.

broth • er   My <u>brother</u> and I help our father clean the house.

bus • y   Annabelle was too <u>busy</u> with her homework to take a walk with me.

buy   I will use my pennies to <u>buy</u> a red ball.

C

cal • en • dar   The <u>calendar</u> shows that my birthday falls on Friday this year.

card   I made a birthday <u>card</u> for my grandmother.

caught   Abe <u>caught</u> the ball with one hand.

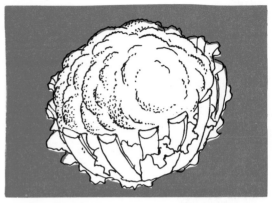

cau • li • flow • ers   Debbie grew <u>cauliflowers</u> last year.

cave   We found an old <u>cave</u> in the side of the mountain.

chased   The dog <u>chased</u> the deer into the woods.

chick • en   The <u>chicken</u> lived on the farm.

cir • cle   We all have to stand in a <u>circle</u> to play this game.

cir • rus   I saw small, white <u>cirrus</u> clouds in the sky this morning.

267

climbed The cat <u>climbed</u> all the way to the top of the tree and wouldn't come down.

close Our house is <u>close</u> to the school.

clouds There were gray <u>clouds</u> in the sky before it rained.

cock·a·doo·dle·doo <u>Cock-a-doodle-doo</u> is the crowing sound a rooster makes.

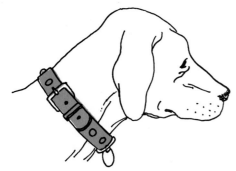

col·lar Sam put a <u>collar</u> on his dog.

col·lec·tion Emmeline has many rocks in her <u>collection</u>.

col·lec·tors Garbage <u>collectors</u> put all the garbage together and take it away.

cook·ies I have milk and <u>cookies</u> when I get home from school.

crow You can hear the rooster <u>crow</u> when the sun comes up.

cu·mu·lus I saw big, white <u>cumulus</u> clouds in the blue sky.

D

de·cid·ed I <u>decided</u> to paint my bike red.

died The flowers <u>died</u> because Butch did not water them.

does·n't The kitten <u>doesn't</u> want to stay in the box.

done The drawings were <u>done</u> with crayons.

drag·on The <u>dragon</u> in the story looks like a big lizard.

draw·ing Beatrix made a <u>drawing</u> of a bamboo shoot.

dry The <u>dry</u>, brown grass needs rain.

268

E

ear·drum   That sound hurts my eardrum!

ears   We use our ears to hear.

earth   You must dig up the earth before you can grow flowers.

el·e·phant   An elephant is a very strong animal.

en·er·gy   Leroy is so full of energy that he runs all the way home.

e·ven   Even if it rains we will go to the park.

eve·ning   The sun goes down in the evening.

ev·er   This is the best doghouse I have ever seen.

eyes   We see with our eyes.

F

fair   I played a game and watched a clown at the fair.

far   So far, I have sold five tickets.

farm   The cows are milked on the farm.

feath·er·y   The white clouds looked soft and feathery.

Feb·ru·ar·y   It snowed a lot this year during February.

felt   I felt the cold wind on my face.

few   There were only a few flowers here last year.

fire   We sat around the fire to get warm.

flopped   Isabel was so tired that she flopped down on the grass after running.

269

fluff   The baby's hair is just like fluff.

for · est   The tree grew in the forest.

for · get   I try to remember to do my homework, but sometimes I forget.

Fri · day   Friday is the day after Thursday.

full   The box was full of pennies.

fur   The dog's fur keeps it warm in winter.

G

ga · rage   Mother drove the car into the garage.

gi · ant   In the story, there was a giant as big as a house.

girls'   The girls' names are Kim and Sally.

giv · ing   The farmer was giving away free rabbits.

glad   I'm glad I am moving to a new town but sad to leave my friends.

good · ness   "My goodness," she cried, when she saw the mouse.

grew   She grew cauliflowers on the farm.

H

hair   That girl has long, brown hair.

hard   Abe rode hard on his bike.

hard · ly   I was so late I hardly had time to eat breakfast.

hatch   The bird is ready to hatch from the egg.

hear   Can you hear the birds singing?

heard   I heard you playing the piano.

hel · lo   I say hello when I see my friends on the playground.

her · self   Ann can read this book all by herself.

high · est   This frog can jump the highest of them all.

hit   Kat hit the ball.

hun · dred   I can count from one to one hundred.

hunt·ing Butch can't find his shoe and is <u>hunting</u> for it now.

hur·ry <u>Hurry</u> up and find your shoes, or we will be late for the play.

I

I'd <u>I'd</u> like to go to the park with you.

i·mag·ine Howard tried to <u>imagine</u> what it would be like to be a fish.

in·vis·i·ble You cannot see things that are <u>invisible</u>.

I've <u>I've</u> seen horses on a farm, but I have never seen ponies.

J

jet A <u>jet</u> flew in the sky.

job Cleaning the house is a hard <u>job</u>.

K

kiss I gave my mother and father a hug and a <u>kiss</u> before bed.

knew I wish I <u>knew</u> the answer.

L

lap When I sat down, the dog jumped into my <u>lap</u>.

la·ter If we do our homework now, we can play <u>later</u>.

laugh The funny clown made me <u>laugh</u>.

law The <u>law</u> says you must keep your dog on a leash.

lay The cat <u>lay</u> on the rug.

leaned Willie and his brother <u>leaned</u> on their bikes as they talked.

learn Fred will <u>learn</u> to read in school this year.

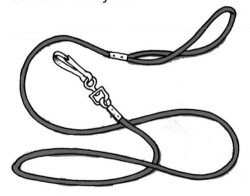

leash John put a <u>leash</u> on the dog to take it for a walk.

lick Cats <u>lick</u> their feet to keep them clean.

light   One room was full of <u>light</u> in the dark house.

lis·ten   <u>Listen</u> to Aunty read the story about dragons.

live   Hal wants a real <u>live</u> rabbit for his birthday.

lone·ly   Bob felt <u>lonely</u> at the new school.

loop   Larry made a <u>loop</u> at the end of the rope.

loud   The drums made a <u>loud</u> noise.

M

mad   I got <u>mad</u> at my dog when it ran away.

ma·gic   The princess used her <u>magic</u> wand to turn the frog into a prince.

main   The <u>main</u> street is the most important street in a city.

mares'   Both <u>mares'</u> colts are brown.

mas·ter   The dog came when its <u>master</u> called.

mat·ter   Winifred wanted to know what was the <u>matter</u> with the sick cat.

mid·dle   Don't ride your bike in the <u>middle</u> of the street.

missed   Rico <u>missed</u> his friend who had moved away.

mis·ter   A man can be called <u>mister</u>.

mon·key   The <u>monkey</u> jumped from branch to branch.

most   <u>Most</u> of the time Joe is happy, but sometimes he is sad.

moun · tain The <u>mountain</u> is so high that clouds hide part of it.

Mr. <u>Mr.</u> Lopez is my teacher.

Mrs. <u>Mrs.</u> Potter is Ken's mother.

mu · sic Can you play that <u>music</u> on the piano?

mu · si · cians The <u>musicians</u> can play the drums as well as the piano.

my · self There was no one to help me, so I did it all by <u>myself</u>.

N

near · ly I <u>nearly</u> forgot your birthday, but I remembered just in time.

nests Those birds lay blue eggs in their <u>nests</u>.

noise That <u>noise</u> sounds like thunder.

O

O.K. Is it <u>O.K.</u> if I use your umbrella?

once I went to the zoo <u>once</u>, but I have been to the park two times.

o · pen The <u>open</u> window let air in the room.

or · der The man next door gave me an <u>order</u> for two boxes of cookies.

own This bike is Hal's, but that bike is my <u>own</u>.

273

P

pa·rade   The elephants marched in the parade.

pen·nies   I can buy a balloon for six pennies.

pet   My pet dog likes to play ball with me.

plants   The plants are growing well by the window.

please   Please help me push this door closed.

po·ems   She liked to read poems about animals.

po·lice of·fi·cers   The police officers found my dog when it ran away.

po·ta·toes   Potatoes grow in the ground.

pret·ty   I don't like that plant, but this one is very pretty.

prob·lem   That old car has always been a problem.

proud·ly   Sandy pointed proudly to the picture he had painted.

puf·fy   The rabbit has a puffy, white tail.

Q

quick   Some dogs are quick to learn and some are slow.

R

read·y   It is time to leave, but I am not ready to go.

real·ly   I cried when I cut my knee because it really hurt.

re·mem·ber   They always remember to put on their shoes, but they sometimes forget to put on their socks.

re·ward   If we find the missing money, we may get a reward.

riv·er We can catch some fish in the river.

rob·ber The police saw the robber take the gold.

roo·ster The rooster crowed in the morning.

row I sit in the last row at school.

sale There are kittens for sale at the pet shop.

sal·ty The fish tastes salty to me.

sam·ples Try the free samples of cookies to see if you like them.

scared The dragon in the story scared me.

sci·en·tist The scientist tried to find out if bluejays lay blue eggs.

scold·ed The teacher scolded the children who forgot their books.

scream·ing The people were screaming at the baseball game.

sent Grandma sent me a card on my birthday.

sev·en I counted seven frogs in the lake.

shall We shall go to the zoo, and then we will eat lunch in the park.

shook Carmen shook the snow off the branch onto the ground.

shoot The shoot of the young plant began to grow.

should You should put a bandage on that cut.

show I will <u>show</u> you how to ride your bike.

sky Birds fly in the <u>sky</u>.

slug A <u>slug</u> ate my potato plant.

smal·ler A kitten is <u>smaller</u> than a cat.

smart Ben has a <u>smart</u> dog that can catch a ball.

spe·cial Mother made a <u>special</u> breakfast on my birthday.

spoon You eat soup with a <u>spoon</u>.

spring We planted beets in the <u>spring</u>, and in the winter we ate them.

start·ed The game <u>started</u> at ten o'clock.

stepped Ben <u>stepped</u> in some water and got his feet wet.

stood When James got tired of sitting, he <u>stood</u> up.

sto·ries Linda writes <u>stories</u> about dragons.

sto·ry The best <u>story</u> is the one about the boy and the giant.

sto·ry·tell·er The <u>storyteller</u> told us about giants.

stra·tus <u>Stratus</u> clouds are low and look like fog.

string The kitten played with some <u>string</u>.

stub·born The donkey was <u>stubborn</u> and wouldn't move.

sum·mer We can swim in the river in the <u>summer</u> but not in the winter.

swamp Alligators can be found in a <u>swamp</u>.

276

T

talk   Kate and Kim <u>talk</u> on the way to school.

tall   This plant was small last year, but now it's <u>tall</u>.

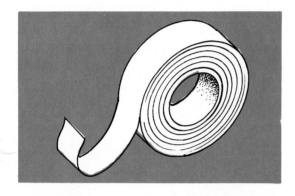

tape   Put some <u>tape</u> on the box to keep it closed.

task   It is a hard <u>task</u> to rake leaves.

taste   We'll eat some ice cream, and then <u>taste</u> the birthday cake.

those   <u>Those</u> are cumulus clouds.

through   The snake crawled <u>through</u> the tall grass.

throw   Ben can <u>throw</u> the ball as far as I can.

thun·der   The sound of <u>thunder</u> makes Sam feel scared.

Thurs·days   <u>Thursdays</u> are special days for Ben.

trav·el·ers   The <u>travelers</u> waited for the boat to take them down the river.

tried   We <u>tried</u> to walk faster.

trot   Horses move fast when they <u>trot</u>.

trucks   We needed two <u>trucks</u> to move our things to the new house.

try   If we <u>try</u> to walk faster, we will not be late.

turn   It is my <u>turn</u> to ride the pony now.

U

un · hap · py   Ted felt sad and unhappy when he couldn't go outside to play.

use   Mindy has no use for the present I gave her.

V

vil · lage   A village is a small town.

W

warm   The soup was still warm from the oven.

wa · ter · mel · ons   Watermelons taste good when it's hot.

we'd   We'd wanted to see you, but we are busy today.

week   There are seven days in a week.

we're   We're going to the lake today, but we don't know what time we will leave.

wheel · chair   People who can't walk use a wheelchair.

wind   The wind blew through the trees.

win · dow   I closed the window to keep out the rain.

wings   Birds use their wings to fly.

wish   I have a fish, but I wish I had a dog.

wo · men   One woman stood by the door, and two women sat in the chairs.

won·der   I <u>wonder</u> what I did with my crayons.

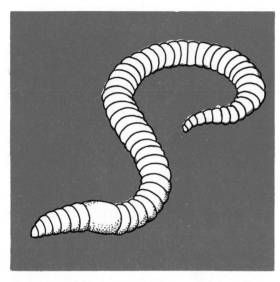

worm   The <u>worm</u> crawls in the wet earth.

yard   My dog likes to play in our <u>yard</u>.

year   I will be eight next <u>year</u>.

years   Ann is seven <u>years</u> old today.

young·est   Chippy is the <u>youngest</u> in a family of six children, and Betsy is the oldest.

you're   <u>You're</u> a good runner, and I'm a good singer.

Z

zoo   We gave peanuts to the elephants at the <u>zoo</u>.

279